Phonemic Awareness Tales

Workbook

Copyright 2004
Second Edition
Printed in U.S.A.

ISBN: 0-9725803-6-0

Written by Lavelle Carlson, M.S., CCC/SLP
Illustrated by Lucas Adams

No portion of this workbook except the specified reproducible pages can be copied.
Pages 93-143

Additional information regarding Phonemic Awareness Tales and/or permission to reprint the non-reproducible pages may be obtained by writing to:

Children's Publishing
201 Woodland Park
Georgetown, Texas 78628
512-864-7364
www.childrenspublishing.com
carlson@cox-internet.com

TABLE OF CONTENTS

Introduction	Page 5
Preface	Page 11
Can a Toucan Hoot Too?	Page 13
Materials	
Familiarization activity	
Vocabulary list	
Activities	
Animal/Environmental sound awareness	
Word awareness	
Syllable awareness	
Speech sound awareness and onset plus rhyme	
The Fable of Mable with the Ladle at the Table	Page 33
Materials	
Familiarization activity	
Vocabulary list	
Activities	
Animal/Environmental sound awareness	
Word awareness	
Syllable awareness	
Speech sound awareness and onset plus rhyme	
Rocks in My Socks and Rainbows Too	Page 51
Materials	
Familiarization activity	
Vocabulary list	
Activities	
Animal/Environmental sound awareness	
Word awareness	
Syllable awareness	
Speech sound awareness and onset plus rhyme	
The Frog Who Could Not Croak	Page 69
Materials	
Familiarization activity	
Vocabulary list	
Activities	
Animal/Environmental sound awareness	
Word awareness	
Syllable awareness	
Speech sound awareness and onset plus rhyme	
References and Suggested Readings	Page 89
Reproducible Pictures	Page 91

INTRODUCTION

In 1994 the International Dyslexia Association adopted the definition of dyslexia that is also used by the National Institute of Child and Health and Human Development (NICHD).

- Specific learning disability that is neurological in origin
- Characterized by difficulties with word recognition, poor spelling and poor decoding abilities that often are the result of a deficit in phonological processing
- May also include problems in reading comprehension
- Lack of reading experience can inhibit growth of vocabulary and background knowledge

Adopted by the IDA Board of Directors, Nov. 12, 2002. This definition is also used by the National Institute of Child Health and Human Development (NICHD).

Approximately 20% (the prevalence varies slightly depending on the source) of the population has dyslexia. In those populations that have less language experiences as a young child the prevalence of reading disabilities may be higher. Research shows that phonological awareness training in the early years will decrease the reading disabilities (NICHD). This notebook addresses the problem in the preschool ages through early elementary.

Many of the reading disabilities can be ameliorated with early intervention. Many educational groups have developed guidelines to address this issue. The Texas guidelines for the pre-kindergarten curriculum in the areas of language and early literacy encompass listening comprehension, speech production and speech discrimination, verbal expression, phonological awareness, print and book awareness, letter knowledge and early word recognition, motivation to read, developing knowledge of literary forms, and written expression (Texas Education Association). For the specific levels refer to the TEA web site: http://www.tea.state.tx.us/curriculum/early/prekguide.html

The skills for successful reading originate early in life when the child begins to hear and process language and sounds. The precursors to the higher reading skills of phonics, vocabulary and comprehension are phonological and phonemic awareness, oral language, and print awareness (NICHD). Although at a higher reading level all the skills work in tandem to produce good readers, phonological awareness is now considered to be the supporting base for early reading (Torgerson et al, 1997). The levels that will be taught after phonological awareness are: phonics (letter to sound correspondence), writing, and spelling (NICHD).

Phonological awareness is the ability to perceive discrete parts of words and manipulate the parts to create new words and increase vocabulary. Two of the important components of phonological awareness (Lindamood, 1975) are:

- Discrimination of likenesses and differences between individual speech sounds.
- Perceive and represent the sameness or difference, number, and order of speech sounds, both in sequences of isolated sounds and in syllable units. The manipulation includes the addition, deletion, substitution, and shifting of sounds to create a new meaningful syllable or word.

(1) Word level example:

- There are six words in the sentence, *The dog is big and brown.*
- I say, *The toucan eats seeds.* Now you help me finish the sentence, *The toucan eats _____.* The student replies *seeds*.
- Finish this sentence. An elephant is big but a mouse is _____. The student replies *little*.

(2) Syllable level example:

- Segment syllables. Break the word *fireman* and you have two meaningful units; i.e., *fire* and *man*.
- Blend separate syllables to say the word; i.e., *fire* (pause) *man* = *fireman*.

At a higher reading level the ability to manipulate syllables greatly increases one's vocabulary.

- *Apart* delete *a* = *part*.
- *Part* add *de* = *depart*.
- *Depart* add *ment* = *department*.
- *Department* substitute *a* for *de* = *apartment*.
- *Apartment* delete *ment* = *apart*.
- *Apart* delete *a* = *part*.
- *Part* add *y* = *party*.

(3) In the onset to rhyme level the initial consonant is changed to be followed by the same vowel sound and any other accompanying sounds.

- /b/ + *ag* = bag.
- /r/ + *ag* = rag.

(4) Sound level is the phonemic awareness level of phonological awareness. Phoneme refers to a speech sound. It is the ability to perceive and manipulate individual speech sounds; i.e. add, delete, shift, substitute, blend, and segment.

- *Mat* delete /m/ = *at*.
- *Mat* add /s/ (sound) = *mats*.
- *Mats* with the /t/ and /s/ (sounds) shifted = *mast*.
- *Mat* with /k/ (sound, letter "c" substituted for /m/ (sound) = *cat*.

- Blending the separate sounds in a word to say the word; i.e., /c/, /a/, /t/ = *cat*.
- Segmenting a word into its separate parts; i.e., *me* = /m/, /e/.

When teaching phonological awareness it is important to keep the instruction at an appropriate level. The suggested teaching sequence is word level, syllable level, onset and rhyme, and phonemic awareness (speech sound) level (Goldsworthy, 1996). The hierarchy of phonological/phonemic awareness instruction in this workbook is:

- Animal/environmental sound awareness
- Word awareness
- Syllable awareness
- Speech sound awareness
- Onset-rhyme (rhyming words) – This is included under speech sound awareness activities.

At the animal/environmental awareness level the students are learning the concepts of identifying and sequencing environmental sounds. This paves the way for understanding the more abstract concepts of identifying and sequencing speech sounds later. This is a good time to teach the concepts "first sound, middle sound, last sound." Try using visual cues left-to-right from the children's perspective. You can have the students making the noise line up left-to-right in front of the class. You can use picture cues on a felt board in the left-to-right progression. As these activities are done, keep in mind that the same activities can be done at a higher level substituting letters and sounds.

Prior to teaching the phonemic awareness skills it is a good idea to have some activities to acquaint the children with the vocabulary. Allow the children to color and cut out reproducible pictures in this workbook and make their own books while talking about the pictures. They can then read their book to one another by turning the pages and telling what is on each page.

If a child is having difficulty with sequencing of words, syllables, or sounds, the hierarchy can be broken into more discrete steps:

- Identify one word.
- Identify and sequence two words.
- Identify and sequence three words.
- Identify one syllable.
- Identify and sequence two syllables.
- Identify and sequence three syllables.
- Identify one sound.
- Identify and sequence two sounds.
- Identify and sequence three sounds.

Phonemic awareness is facilitated by hands-on activities. Prior to teaching sequencing of letters and graphemes use colored blocks, felt squares or other manipulatives. To use felt squares put up the number and colors of squares corresponding to the number of sounds and sameness/difference. For the word *moo* use two squares of different colors to be placed on two spots. For the word *dove* use three squares of different colors to be placed on three spots. For *baby* use four squares with #1 for /b/ and #3 for /b/ of the same color. Either add or omit a square depending on whether a sound is added or omitted. The same would apply for the number and sameness/difference of syllables.

An effective multisensory method to teach syllable recognition is to use a mirror to watch the hand held under the chin going up and down with each syllable. Another fun method of teaching this is to give the child a mini M & M each time the chin drops while saying a word. Count the number of M & M's earned. You can also have the children drop blocks in a box for each time the chin drops. Mice castanets can also be used to give additional auditory and visual feedback on counting at the syllable level as well as the word and speech sound levels.

Although phonological awareness is considered to be the supporting base for reading, teaching the language skills and language concepts that are important to comprehension can facilitate it. Some of the language concepts and terms that will be used later; i.e., beginning, middle, end, can be taught using environmental and animal sounds initially, then progressing to the letters and letter sounds and sound/symbol correspondence. At this time the terms that will be used later can be introduced. Some of the questions to ask in this section are:

- Where is the (_____) sound?
- Is it at the beginning, in the middle, or at the end (of a sequence of sounds)? If there are two or more students making a sequence of sounds, it is best to have them stand left-to-right from the observing students' perspective.
- What do you see? Response: cow.
- What sound does the cow make? Response: Moo.

At a higher level; i.e., sound/symbol correspondence, the last two questions will later be posed as:

- What letter(s) do you see? Response: b.
- "What sound do you hear (does the letter say)?" Response: /b/ (Slash represents sound.)

Print awareness is another skill that works along with phonological awareness to ensure reading success. This includes concepts such as alphabet knowledge (Worden and Boettcher, 1990), left-to-right directionality, and literacy terms; i.e., letter and word. When addressing phonological awareness through storybook reading remember to address the other skills that are also important for reading; i.e. print awareness. Talk about the front of the book, the back of the book and the title of the book while pointing to the words in the title. Indicate left-to-right progression by using your finger. Indicate that words represent an image by pointing to the words which are imbedded in the pictures.

The exercises in this manual deal more with the manipulation of the sounds. For those needing to know which sounds are more developmentally appropriate for production, Pro-Ed, Austin, Texas sells a comprehensive speech and language chart.

In recent years speech pathologists have been using shared storybook reading to facilitate both language and phonemic awareness skills to increase generalization and relevance of the skills being taught. Storybook reading facilitates the speech goals and, at the same time, facilitates the academic goals of emergent literacy. Paired reading and echo reading (Robertson, 2002) as well as related activities are a great way to achieve this generalization.

For those at greatest risk teaching phonemic awareness explicitly derived greater benefits than incidental teaching (Torgerson, et al, 1997). How can the levels of phonological processing be taught explicitly without sacrificing the benefits derived from teaching in natural contexts?

With careful planning and practice there can be a balance between the explicit teaching of phonemic awareness and the naturalistic contexts of storybooks. The storybook should be used as the basis for incorporating phonemic awareness around themed activities. If the story is about a toucan, develop a rainforest theme and activities. Use the activities throughout the day. During art make rain sticks, masks and a rainforest theatre to use during drama time. Talk about the sounds. Play CDs with the sounds. Have the children participate in sound activities during movement activities. For example, when you have the students move from one activity to another, speak phrases from the book and have the students take a step for each word as you say it. If you say, "A toucan can hoot," they take four steps. Have a sound for the day or for the week. Put a picture board up with two vertical columns, one for the initial sound and one for the end sound. At the top of the each column put the letter representing the sound. Throughout the day or week allow the children to put pictures beginning with the sound in the left column and those ending with the sound in the right column. Have the children participate in rhyming activities throughout the day.

There are some children who are not interested in books. For the children who have difficulty attending to the entire reading of the book encourage participation in other ways. During activities make references to the book and have them refer to it to locate a picture of what you are talking about. Try to incorporate movement and activities in the story to begin building the interest of the children who have a short attention span. For those who are at greatest risk work with them in a smaller group to allow more practice and greater success at each level prior to going to the next level.

While working with the young child, always be cognizant of the differences in dialects of minorities and discrimination in English from *second language learners*. One factor affecting Spanish-English bilingual speakers' discrimination is the absence of some of the English vowels in Spanish. This results in confusion in discrimination (Flege, 1991) such as "dock/duck," "suit/soot," "bed/bid," "beck/back," "gnat/knot."

Books appropriate for the emerging and early literacy should have text embedded in the pictures, be repetitive, and have large print. The story should be of a length that matches the attention span of the children. Try to choose stories that lend themselves to comprehension questions of who, what, where, when, and how. However, when asking these comprehension questions, use methods that ensure the children are comfortable in responding. To use a non-evaluative method of questioning use a hierarchy from yes/no questions to choice questions to direct (What?) questions.

- Can a toucan hoot? If the children are unsure how to respond, you shake your head indicating no. The children will then respond no.
- Does a toucan hoot or say ku-ya-ke-ke? By giving the correct answer last the children are more likely to provide that answer.
- What does a toucan say? By the time you have reached this level of questioning the children should be able to respond *ku-ya-ke-ke*.

If you are an early childhood teacher and are uncertain if a child simply has a delay that will be ameliorated with regular classroom intervention or if the child may require more direct intervention, consult your speech pathologist for a screening or a full assessment.

PREFACE

The Phonemic Awareness Tales were written to meet the requirements of early childhood programs in a fun and stimulating way (Texas Education Association). They are excellent resources for parents, early childhood teachers, speech pathologists, and English as *second language learners*.

The Phonemic Awareness Tales Workbook is intended for Head Start, pre-kindergarten, kindergarten, and first grade, depending on the child's skill level. The exercises in this workbook are to be used in conjunction with the Phonemic Awareness Tales. The repetition and predictability in these stories can also facilitate speech and language in children diagnosed with autism and developmental apraxia of speech. The stories can also be used for generalization of articulation skills. Although some of these activities may be original with the author, many are adaptations of activities that the author learned from other speech pathologists over the years. It is hoped that this workbook and the accompanying books provide speech pathologists, teachers, and parents with additional useful activities to add to their repertoire of knowledge and materials.

Current research indicates that phonological awareness is a crucial skill for ensuring that children learn the skill of reading. Today reading is more important than ever for success in a world that depends on written communication. It is important to remember that there are always exceptions. There may be children who do not have superior phonological awareness skills but have other strengths that compensate in reading. It is also possible to have superior phonological awareness skills but have poor comprehension skills (Asperger's Syndrome).

Phonological awareness in and of itself is not the answer for happiness and success. It is important to appreciate persons who may have a neurological deficit that precludes learning to read well. Each person has a unique gift and contribution to make. It is hoped that is what teachers and speech pathologists will bring out in children.

Thanks to Lucas Adams for providing the artwork in this workbook.

CAN A TOUCAN HOOT TOO?

ACTIVITIES

Materials

A. Exercises – included
B. Reproducible animal masks – included
C. Small reproducible pictures of animals – included
D. Rainforest scene reproducible – included
E. Rainforest theatre (see instructions and reproducible pictures)
F. Fan (optional) – not included
G. Coconut (split and with coconut milk saved in plastic container) – not included
H. Shredded coconut placed in the split coconut – not included
I. Picture of orchid (reproducible) – included
J. Vanilla bean or picture of bean – not included
K. Bottle of vanilla extract – not included
L. Leaves – included. These can be colored from the reproducible and attached to a stick or purchased at a hobby store. During the activity you can sprinkle water on the children to simulate water dropping off rainforest canopy.
M. CD with rainforest sounds if available
N. Instructions for student-made rainstick, student-made butterflies, rainforest display

    1. Student-made rainstick: Using a long wrapping paper tube, hammer drywall nails into the tube randomly. Fill it with about ½ cup rice. Seal the end of the tube with paper (fairly heavy-weight paper works best) taped on with masking tape. The tube can be decorated with tissue paper glued to the tube.

    2. Student-made butterflies: Use one pipe cleaner and colored tissue paper. Fold the pipe cleaner once. Twist the two ends around each other except for a quarter inch on one end. Allow this end to serve as the two antennae. Cut oval or rectangular strips of the tissue paper and twist the pipe cleaner around the center with the two ends protruding on the top for the antennae.

    3. Class-made rainforest display: Allow the children to color the rainforest display reproducible. Glue these to mat board, display board, or a cardboard box (with one side open). For the trees, cut branches out of brown construction paper and the leaves out of green construction paper or allow the children to color the leaves. Glue the trunks, branches, and leaves on all sides and the top (rainforest canopy) of the inside. Make brown leaves for the students to put on the floor of the rainforest. Have the students draw and color snakes and spiders to put in the rainforest.

O. Optional purchases:
    (Contact Children's Publishing for ordering information.)
        Toucan puppet
        Wooden frog with dowel (creates true frog sound)
        Wooden cricket with dowel (creates true cricket sound)
        Thunder tube
        Rainstick
        Rainforest CD

P. Recipe for coconut macaroons
   Ingredients:
   2 egg whites
   Dash salt
   ½ teaspoon vanilla
   2/3 cup granulated sugar
   1 - 3 ½ oz. can (1 1/3 cups) flaked coconut

Beat egg whites with dash salt and the vanilla until soft peaks form. Gradually add sugar, beating until stiff. Fold in coconut. Drop by teaspoons onto greased cookie sheet. Bake at 325 degrees 20 minutes.

Vocabulary Familiarization Activity

1. Color the rainforest pictures and hang them on the wall to resemble a rainforest or have a small rainforest theatre per instructions in Materials section. Place these items on a table in front of the display: (1) coconut with shredded coconut (2) coconut milk (3) picture of colored orchid with vanilla bean taped on picture (4) bottle of vanilla extract next to orchid (5) pictures of rainforest animals and birds [reproducible section] (6) wooden crickets and frogs (7) thunder tube (8) toucan puppet.

Feeling:
    Wind (fan) – Talk about fast and slow.
    Water (rain) – Tell the children (sitting in a circle) that you will go around and sprinkle them with water from the leaves while their eyes are closed and they are to pretend they are in a rainforest. Tell them to feel the raindrops. Talk about wet/dry and cold/warm.
    Coconut – Allow the children to feel the moist coconut on the inside of the shell and the hard outer shell. Talk about wet/dry, hard/soft, smooth/rough and hairy.

Hearing:
    Thunder, frogs, crickets, toucan – Demonstrate all the sounds before the children close their eyes so they will not be frightened. Then, have them close their eyes. Make the various sounds and let the children guess the sounds. Allow the children to make the sounds with the frogs and crickets.

Tasting:
    Coconut, vanilla, coconut macaroons

Smelling:
    Coconut, vanilla

Seeing:
    Orchid, vanilla bean, vanilla extract, animals, birds, butterflies, trees

2. Put on a rainforest concert. Give each child a noisemaker (if you have more than one of each); i.e. small frog, medium frog, large frog, cricket, squeaking toucan, thunder tube. Group the same instruments together. Make a sign for each. Be sure to distinguish between the small, medium, and large frogs by enlarging the pictures. Put the name under each. Allow the children to practice making the noise first. Next, tell the children you will hold up a sign and those children who have that instrument will play it. When the children understand, hold up pictures of two instruments, then three. Last, have a complete rainforest concert by having all the instruments played at the same time.

3. Read the book on several occasions. Tell the children they will help you put on a play. The children can make finger puppets with the small pictures by coloring and cutting them out. Tape them to their finger. As you read the story the children will fill in the repetitive dialogue (with your help) and pretend their character is saying the dialogue.

Vocabulary List

rain	leaves	geckos (lizard)
toucan	trees	spiders
frogs (toads)	snakes	insects
butterflies	monkeys	beetles
canopy	caterpillar	palm(s)
three-toed sloth	lily(ies)	bird(s)
fig(s)	flowers	ant(s)
bats	gorillas	elephants
moth	book	bat(s)
ghost	shoe(s)	cow(s)
dove(s)	owl(s)	flute(s)
moo(s)	coo(s)	hoot(s)
horse(s)	shoo(s)	fly(ies)
boo	baby	Grampy
goo-goo	can	coconut

Vocabulary by Sound

/l/ Initial: leaves, lilies, lizard
   Medial: lilies, gorilla, elephant
   Final: owl, beetle

/g/ Initial: geckos, ghost, gorilla, Grampy, goo-goo
   Medial: goo-goo
   Final: frog, fig

/t/ Initial: toucan, trees
   Medial: butterflies, beetles, caterpillar, three-toed sloth
   Final: ant, bat, ghost

/k/ Initial: canopy, caterpillar, cow, coo, can, coconut
   Medial: gecko, toucan, coconut, monkey
   Final: snake, book

/b/ Initial: bird, book, bat, book, baby
   Medial: baby

/d/ Initial: do, dove
   Medial: spider
   Final: bird, toad

/n/ Medial: canopy
   Final: can, toucan

/m/ Initial: moo, monkey, moth
   Medial: Grampy

Animal/Environmental Sound Awareness Activities

Locate the sound

Activity:

Materials: Reproducible masks

> Instructions: Have one student take an animal/person picture from the box. Tell the other students to close their eyes while the student with the picture hides and then makes the sound of the animal/person represented by the picture. The other students can open their eyes and then tell where the animal/person is located.
>
> Variation: Have the students use noise toys; i.e., croaking wooden frog, rain stick, or chirping wooden cricket.

Activity:

Materials: Reproducible pictures of animals and persons

> Instructions: Divide the class in half. One half is given one picture from one stack. Have this half stand on one side of the room. The other half is given one picture from the other stack. They stand on the opposite side of the room. The first group listens while the second group makes the sounds of their animal/person. (It is best to allow one student at a time to make a sound. However, when the students are familiar with the game, you can then increase the level of difficulty by allowing two or three students to make their sound at the same time.) Students from the first group will then go to the person making the sound of his/her picture. Alternate and allow the second group to listen while the first group makes the sounds.

Identify the sounds

Activity:

Materials: Puppet with noisemaker in beak
          Wooden frog noisemaker
          Wooden cricket noisemaker
          Rainstick (see instructions for making under materials)

> Instructions: Have one student stand a behind screen and make one noise with any of the above noisemakers. The other students then guess what it is. If you are using the frog and cricket, it will be necessary to practice because differentiating between the two may be difficult depending on the age.

Identify the sounds and their position left to right

Activity:

Materials: Small pictures of animals/persons (included in manual)

> Instructions: Have three students stand in front of class. Standing children take a picture card but do not show it to seated children. Tell the children when you tap them (always in a left-to-right progression from the seated children's perspective), they then make their noise. Question to ask: What sound did you hear at the beginning, in the middle, at the end?

Same/different sounds

Activity:

Materials: Pictures

> Instructions: Have two children come to the front. Give each a picture, sometimes the same pictures and sometimes different pictures. Have each student say the animal sound. Ask the seated students if the sound is same or different.

Count the animal/person sounds

Activity:

Materials: Pictures of animals and sometimes a blank card

> Instructions: Tell the children they are to count the sounds. Have four students come to the front in a line. Give each one a paper with an animal picture or a blank card. Tap the students' shoulders left-to-right again. The students say his/her animal sound but the student(s) with blank card(s) says nothing. There may be times when one student is not tapped and, therefore, does not make a sound. At that point explain that only two sounds were heard but three animals were seen.

Teacher: How many sounds did you hear?

Word Awareness Activities

Count the words

Activity:

> Instructions: Tell the children you will say a sentence and they are to tell you how many words are in the sentence. Initially, it is good to use manipulatives, i.e., blocks, felt squares, etc., and/or physical movements; i.e., clapping, hopping, stepping on squares, etc. If necessary, pause between the words until the students understand the concept. This activity can be done easily during the reading of the story once the children are familiar with the dialogue.

    Grampy, Grampy. (2)
    I hear you. (3)
    A dove says "coo." (4)
    Can a toucan hoot too? (5)

Listen for words

Activity:

Materials: None

> Instructions: Tell the children that Simon will say something silly. They are to clap when Simon says the sentence silly (incorrectly). The children should then tell Simon what he should say.

    A cow says hoot. Response: moo.
    A dove says coo. Response: none.
    A flute tooter says moo. Response: toot.
    A ghost says goo-goo. Response: boo.
    A baby says moo. Response: goo-goo.
    A ghost says boo. Response: none.

Listen for words

Activity:

Materials: None

> Instructions: Tell the children that you will say some words. When they hear the name of an animal, make the sound of that animal.

    Cow. Response: moo.
    Chair. Response: none.
    Owl. Response: hoot.
    House. Response: none.

Listen for same or different words

Activity: Pictures, if necessary

Materials: None

> Instructions: Tell the children that you will say some words and they are to tell you if they are same or different.

Teacher: Are these words the same or different?

    Toucan, toucan. Response: same.
    Dove, horse. Response: different.

Listen for missing words in a sequence of words

Activity:

Materials: Pictures of animals – optional
          Felt Squares – optional

> Instructions: Tell the children you will say some words. Then you will say them again and they are to tell you which word you forgot to say. In the beginning it is best to use pictures. Put the pictures on a felt board. Remove the pictures as you say the words. Then put up the pictures in the same order but with one missing. The students should tell you the missing picture. When the children are familiar with the activity, eliminate the use of the pictures and use felt squares or only say the words depending on how successful you feel the children will be.

    Cow, dove, horse. Cow, (clap), horse. Response: dove.
    Toucan, cow, ghost. (clap), cow, ghost. Response: toucan.
    Horse, baby, dove, ghost. Horse, baby, (clap), ghost. Response: dove.

Listen for missing words in a sentence

Activity:

Materials: None

> Instructions: Tell the children you will say a sentence two times and they are to help you by telling you what word you left out the second time. This can also be done during the reading of the repetitive passages. Occasionally, pause and let the children finish the sentence.

    A cow can moo. A cow can (moo).
    A flute tooter can toot a flute. A flute tooter can toot a (flute).
    A baby says goo-goo. A baby says (goo-goo).
    Let's go to the rainforest. Let's go to the (rainforest).

Listen for a different word out of a 3-word sequence

Activity:

Materials: Pictures – optional

> Instructions: Tell the children you will say three words. They are to tell you the word that is different.

    Dove, horse, dove. Response: horse.
    Toucan, ghost, ghost. Response: toucan.

Blend words to create compound words

Activity:

Materials: Pictures – raindrop, raincloud, rainbow
               tin can, toucan

> Instructions: Tell the children you will try to trick them by saying words slow in your robotic voice. They are to guess what you said. Put pictures of similar compound words on the felt board. Say the word with a pause between; i.e., rain-pause-cloud. This helps the students listen for the remainder of the word while becoming aware of using parts to create new words.

    Rain (pause) forest. Response: Rainforest.
    Rain (pause) drop. Response: Raindrop.
    Rain (pause) cloud. Response: Raincloud.

Tou (pause) can. Response: Toucan.
Tin (pause) can. Response: Tin can.

Syllable Awareness Activities

Count the syllables

Activity:

Materials: Vocabulary list
          Mirror if necessary
          M & M's (CAUTION: BE CAREFUL OF ANY WHO HAVE ALLERGIES TO PEANUTS!)

> Instructions: Tell the children you will say a word and they are to tell you how many syllables (how many times their chin moves) are in the word.

    Toucan (2)
    Cow (1)
    Butterflies (3)
    Monkey (2)
    Ghost (1)
    Bird (1)
    Elephant (3)

Delete a syllable

Activity:

Materials: Pictures – optional
          Vocabulary list

> Instructions: Tell the children you will say a word. Then the children are to tell you the word with a part missing.

    Say toucan. Response: toucan. Now say it without -can. Response: tou-.
    Say toucan. Response: toucan. Now say it without tou-. Response: -can.

Add a missing syllable

Activity:

Materials: Pictures – optional
          Ball

> Instructions: Explain that you will say a part of a word and the children are to guess what the word is. Put three or four pictures on the board for the children to choose from. Once the children are familiar with the words you use, discontinue using the pictures. On this you can roll a ball as you say the first syllable(s) and the child to whom the ball is rolled will say the last syllable.

Gram(py), Mon(key), Spi(der), Ge(cko), Caterpi(llar)

Blend syllables to create words

Activity:

Materials: Pictures – optional
Vocabulary list

> Instructions: Tell the children you will say some syllables in a robotic voice and they are to guess the word.

Tou (pause) can. Response: toucan
Ca (pause) ter (pause) pi (pause) llar. Response: caterpillar
Gram (pause) py. Response: Grampy
Ge (pause) cko. Response: gecko
Spi (pause) der. Response: spider
E (pause) le (pause) phant: elephant

Speech Sound Awareness

Materials: Vocabulary list

Count the sounds

Activity:

Materials: Pictures initially or felt squares

> Instructions: Tell the children you will say some speech sounds and they are to tell you how many you said. Use manipulatives and physical movements; i.e. clapping. If necessary, drop tokens in a box and count them after the response. If you use felt squares, place a square for each sound and make them different colors for different sounds.

    M – oo. 2 squares of different colors
    D – o – ve. 3 squares of different colors
    B – a – b – y. 4 squares, square 1 and 3 will be the same color representing /b/ sound.

Listen for same or different initial sounds

Activity:

Materials: Vocabulary list

> Instructions: Tell the children you will say two words. They are to tell you if the first sounds in the words are same or different.

    Boo – ghost. Response: different.
    Moo – man. Response: same.
    Coo – toucan. Response: different.

Listen for missing sounds

Activity:

Materials: Felt squares – optional
          Vocabulary list

> Instructions: Tell the children you will say a word two times. The second time you say it you will forget a sound. They are to tell you what sound did you forgot? Remember to give the sound and not the letter. If you use the felt squares place the same number of squares as sounds on the board. First, say the word, then remove the square representing the sound you omitted.

Moo. (Clap) – oo. Response: /m/.
Cow. (Clap) – ow. Response: /k/.
Ghost. (Clap) – ost. Response: /g/.

Listen for initial sounds /k/, /g/, /t/, /d/

Activity:

Materials: Letter cards

> Instructions: To begin familiarizing the children with sound/symbol association, place the letter representing the targeted sound on the board. Tell the children you will say some words. When they hear the targeted sound at the beginning of the word, they are to clap their hands. Mix words with and without initial targeted sound in each grouping. Use the vocabulary list or any words you feel appropriate.

Targeted sound is /k/.

Cow. Response: clap.
Tree. Response: none.
Coo. Response: clap.

Other stimulus words:
Initial /k/ sound: coo, horse, can, cow, caterpillar
Initial /g/ sound: Grampy, goo-goo, ghost, dove
Initial /t/ sound: shoe, toot, toucan, tree, baby (Randomly insert words that do not begin with targeted sound.)

Omit the initial sound in a word containing only two or three sounds

Activity:

Materials: One- and two-syllable

> Instructions: Explain to the children that you want them to leave out the first sound in some words. Use only words containing 2 or three sounds. Place the same number of squares on the board as sounds represented. Remove the first colored square as the children say the last sounds(s).

Say moo. Response: moo.
Now say moo without the /m/. Response: /oo/.
Say dove. Response: dove.
Teacher: Now say dove without /d/. Response: /ove/.

See vocabulary list for additional stimulus words.

Add an initial sound

Activity:

Materials: Vocabulary list

> Instructions: Explain that you will say a sound or part of a word and the children are to change the word by adding a sound to the beginning.

Say oo. Response: oo.
Now say oo with /m/ at the beginning. Response: moo.
Say at. Response: at.
Now say at with /b/ at the beginning. Response: bat.
Say an. Response: an.
Now say an with /k/ at the beginning. Response: can.

Substitute an initial sound

Activity:

Materials: Vocabulary list

> Instructions: Explain that you will say a word and the children are to change the first sound to make a new word.

Say cow. Response: Cow.
Now say cow but use the sound /n/ in place of /k/. Response: now.
Say boo. Response: boo.
Now say boo but use /sh/ in place of the /b/. Response: shoe.
Say hoot. Response: hoot.
Now say hoot but use /b/ in place of the /h/. Response: boot.

Listen for final sounds /t, g, d/

Activity:

Materials: None

> Instructions: I will say some words. When you hear the targeted sound at the end of the word, say the sound. Mix words with and without final targeted sound in each grouping. Use vocabulary list. To begin sound-letter association put the letter representing the targeted sound on the board.

Targeted sound /t/:

Log. Response: none.
Tree. Response: none.
Bat. Response: clap.
Flute. Response: clap.

See vocabulary list for additional stimulus words.

Omit the final sound in a word

Activity:

Materials: Pictures – optional
Felt squares – optional

> Instructions: Explain that you want them to leave out the last sound in some words. Use only words containing 4 or less sounds. Use squares representing each sound. When the children respond, remove the last felt representing the sound omitted. You can also talk about the number of sounds during this activity.

Say, hoot. Response: hoot.
Now say hoot without the /t/. Response: who.

Hoop – who.
Toad – toe.
Flute – flu.
Moon – moo.
Shoot – shoo.
Boot – boo.

Add the final sound

Activity:

Materials: One-syllable words from vocabulary list
         Pictures – optional

> Instructions: Tell the children you will tell them a sound. Then you will say part of a word and they are to finish the word with their sound when you roll a ball to them.

Say flue. Response: flue.
Teacher: Now say flue with /t/ at the end.
Response: Flute.

Who – hoot.
Toe – toad.
Flu – flute.
Moo – moon.
Shoo – shoot.
Boo – boot.

Substitute a final sound

Activity:

Materials: Vocabulary list

> Instructions: Explain that you will say a word and the children are to change the last sound to a different sound to make a new word.

Say cow. Response: cow.
Now say cow but use the sound /ee/ in place of /oi/.
Response: Key.
Say dove. Response: dove.
Teacher: Now say dove but use /k/ in place of the /v/. Response: Duck.

Horse – horn.
Hoot – hoop.
Bat – bad.
Bat – back.
Bat – bag.
Bat – bam.

Onset-rhyme

Activity:

Materials: None

Instructions:

Teacher: Do these words rhyme?

    Moo – tree? Response: no.
    Moo – coo? Response: yes.
    Tooter – hooter? Response: yes.
    Cow – horse? Response: no.
    Hoot – toot? Response: yes.
    Shoo – moo? Response: yes.

Blend sounds to create words

Activity:

Materials: None

> Instructions: Tell the children you will speak like a robot and they are to guess what you say. Speak with a short pause between each sound. If this is an easy task for the students, make the pauses longer or choose longer words.

    M – oo. Response: moo.
    Gh – o – s – t. Response: ghost.
    D – o – ve. Response: dove.
    H – or – s. Response: horse.

See vocabulary list for additional stimulus words.

THE FABLE OF MABLE WITH THE LADLE AT THE TABLE

ACTIVITIES

Materials

A. Exercises
B. Animal masks – reproducible – goat, goose, moose, bear, ghost, hen
C. Small reproducible pictures of animals/food – reproducible
D. Paper plates to decorate and put pictures of food on during activities
E. Class made menus – Fold 8 ½ by 11" papers in half, the number depends on how many rhyming words you plan to use. Staple the left of the menu to make it the form of a book. On the front write "Child's (name of child) Menu. Allow children to color and decorate their menu.
F. Draw a table on a poster display. Put pictures of foods on it when you talk about them. Always label pictures to teach print awareness. Put pictures of non-foods to the side of the table.

Vocabulary Familiarization Activity

1. Have the children make a menu (See E above). On each left hand page write, "I can eat." On each right page write, "I cannot eat." You can also make a smiley face on the left hand page and a frowning face on the right hand page. Allow the children to color and cut out the foods and accompanying rhyming words; i.e. egg-leg. Have the children glue the picture they can eat on the left hand page. Have the children glue the picture they cannot eat on the right hand page. Allow each child to read his/her menu.

2. Have the children bring in their favorite cereal boxes. Put these on a bulletin board under the heading "Breakfast." Allow them to make rhyming words with their cereal; i.e. Cheerios, Feerios, etc.

3. Allow the students to act out the parts in the book with the teacher or speech therapist being Mable. You will read your part and each child will read a part of the character. They can make signs with the print of their part. Even if they cannot read it, they should be able to remember their part after a couple of readings of the book. You can also help those children who do not remember their part.

Vocabulary List

cake, snake
bear, pear
beans, jeans
peas, fleas, cheese, keys
bread, bed
fable, Mable, table
cape, grape, tape
corn, horn
mice, rice, nice
egg, leg
ghost, toast, post, roast
goose, moose, juice
hen, pen
ladle
roadrunner

Additional food related vocabulary for phonological awareness activities:

black, blackberries
blue, blueberries
straw, strawberries
tomatoes, potatoes
ice, ice cream, ice cube
cheese, cheeseburger, hamburger, ham
lunch, crunch, munch
sand, sandwich
goats, oats

Vocabulary by Sound

/k/ Initial: cake, crunch, can, cape, corn, keys
    Final: cake, snake, black

/b/ Initial: bear, beans, bees, black, blue, bread, bed
    Medial: fable, Mable, table

/p/ Initial: pear, peas, pan, post, pen
    Final: cape, grape, tape

/g/ Initial: grape, ghost, goose
    Final: egg, leg

/m/ Initial: Mable, meat, moose

/t/ Initial: tape, table
   Final: meat, feet, eat, toast, post, roast (the last three may be difficult to perceive when coarticulated with /s/

/s/ Initial: snake
   Final: ice, mice, nice, goose, moose, juice

/z/ Final: fleas, bees, cheese

Animal/Environmental Sound Awareness Activities

Locate the sound

Activity:

Materials: Noisemakers – pan, wooden ladle

Activity:

> Instructions: Give one child the ladle and pan. While the other children close their eyes s/he goes to another part of the room and makes the noise. The other children then guess the location of the noise.

Count the sounds

Activity:

Materials: Ladle, pan

> Instructions: Tell the children you will beat and they will eat. Tell them you will beat on the pan with the ladle (1-4 times) and they are to help you count the beats. For a special treat you can put miniature marshmallows out and have an assistant help the children take the same number of marshmallows as your beat. Eat them and then beat and eat again.

Word Awareness Activities

Count the words

Activity:

> Instructions: Tell the children you will say a sentence and they are to tell you how many words you said. Initially, it is good to use manipulatives, i.e., blocks, felt squares, etc., and/or physical movements; i.e. clapping, hopping, stepping on squares, etc. If necessary, pause between the words until the students understand the concept. When listening for the number of words in sentences it may be necessary for you to give longer pauses between words. This can be done easily during the reading of the story once the children are familiar with the dialogue.

    Good choice! (2)
    Please be nice. (3)
    Do not eat me! (4)
    Boys do not eat fleas. (5)

Listen for words

Activity:

Materials: None

> Instructions: Tell the children that Simon will say something silly. The children should then tell Simon what he should say.

    Boys eat fleas. Response: No, boys eat peas.
    Boys eat snakes. Response: Boys eat cake.
    Eat a bear. Response: Eat a pear.
    Eat keys. Response: Eat cheese.
    Eat a ghost. Response: Eat toast.

Listen for words

Activity:

Materials: None

Instructions: Tell the children that you will say some words. When they hear the name of a food, say "m-m good."

> Cheese. Response: m-m good.
> Snake. Response: none.
> Pear. Response: m-m good.
> Mice. Response: none.

Listen for same or different words

Activity: Pictures, if necessary

Materials:

Instructions: Tell the children that you will say some words and they are to tell you if they are same or different.

> Keys, keys. Response: same.
> Cheese, snake. Response: different.

Listen for missing words in a sequence of words

Activity:

Materials: Pictures – optional

Instructions: Tell the children you will say some words. Then you will say them again and they are to tell you the word you forgot to say. In the beginning it is best to use pictures. Put the pictures on a felt board. Remove the pictures as you say the words. Then put up the pictures in the same order but with one missing. The students should tell you the missing picture. Once the children understand the activity discontinue the use of pictures.

> Snake, pear, mice. Snake, (clap), mice
>   Response: pear
> Ghost, grape, beans. (clap), grape, beans.
>   Response: ghost
> Jeans, corn, rice, keys. Jeans corn, (clap), keys
>   Response: rice

Listen for missing words in a sentence

Activity:

Materials: None

> Instructions: Tell the children you will say a sentence two times. The second time you will leave out a word and they are to help you by telling you what word you left out.

    Good morning, Mable with a ladle.
    Good morning, Mable with a _____. Response: ladle.
    Girls do not eat a horn. Girls blow a horn.
    Girls do not eat a horn. Girls blow a _____. Response: horn.

Listen for a different word out of a 3-word sequence

Activity:

Materials: None

> Instructions: Tell the children you will say three words and they are to tell you which word is different.

    Peas, book, peas. Response: book.
    Mable, Mable, cheese. Response: cheese.
    Mice, mice, corn. Response: corn.
    Peas, peas, cake. Response: cake.

Blend words to create compound words

Activity:

Materials: None

> Tell the children you will try to trick them. You will say a word slowly in your robotic voice and they are to guess what it is.

    Ham (pause) burger. Response: hamburger
    Cheese (pause) burger. Response: cheeseburger
    Cat (pause) fish. Response: catfish
    Straw (pause) berry. Response: strawberry
    Sand (pause) wich. Response: sandwich

Syllable Awareness Activities

Count the syllables

Activity:

Materials: Vocabulary list
Mirror if necessary
M & M's (CAUTION: BE CAREFUL OF ANY WHO HAVE ALLERGIES TO PEANUTS!)

> Instructions: Tell the children you will say a word and they are to tell you how many syllables (how many times their chin moves) are in the word.

    Apple (2)
    Cheeseburger (3)
    Beans (1)
    Mable (2)
    Table (2)
    Cake (1)

Delete a syllable

Activity:

Materials: Pictures – optional
Vocabulary list

> Instructions: Tell the children you will say a word. Then the children are to tell you the word with a part missing.

Say Mable. Response: Mable. Now say it without -ble. Response: Ma-.
    Say Mable. Response: Mable. Now say it without Ma-. Response: -ble.
    Say roadrunner. Response: roadrunner. Now say it without road-. Response: runner.
    Say roadrunner. Response: roadrunner. Now say it without runner. Response: road.

Add a missing syllable

Activity:

Materials: Ball

> Instructions: Explain that you will say a part of a word and the children are to guess what the word is. Give a clue; i.e. I am thinking of a fruit that is yellow and long. It is a bana(final syllable omitted). On this you can roll a ball as you say the first syllable(s) and the child to whom the ball is rolled will say the last syllable; i.e. na.

Bana(na), ta(ble), toma(toes), sand(wich), nap(kin), roadrun(ner), strawber(ry)

Blend syllables to create words

Activity:

Materials: Pictures – optional
Vocabulary list

> Instructions: Tell the children you will say some syllables in a robotic voice and they are to guess the word.

Ma (pause) ble. Response: Mable
Ap (pause) ple. Response: apple
Ba (pause) na (pause) na. Response: banana
Ta (pause) ble. Response: table
La (pause) dle. Response: ladle

Speech Sound Awareness

Count the sounds

Activity:

Materials: Pictures initially or felt squares

Instructions: Tell the children you will say some sounds and they are to tell you how many you said. Use manipulatives and physical movements; i.e. clapping. If necessary, drop tokens in a box and count them after the response. If you use felt squares, place a square for each sound and make them different colors for different sounds. Tell the children you will say some sounds and they are to tell you how many you say.

      B – ee. 2 squares of different colors
      Ch – ee – se. 3 squares of different colors
      M – a – b – le. 4 squares of different colors
      B – e – d. 3 squares of different colors

Listen for same or different initial sounds

Activity:

Materials: Vocabulary list

Instructions: Tell the children you will say two words. Tell if the first sounds in the words are same or different.

      Cat – bed. Response: different.
      Corn – cup. Response: same.
      Bees – goose. Response: different.

Listen for missing sounds

Activity:

Materials: Pictures – optional
          Felt squares
          Vocabulary list

> Instructions: Tell the children you will say a word. Say it again but omit a sound. What sound did I forget? Remember to give the sounds and not the letter. If you use the felt squares place the same number of squares as sounds on the board. First, say the word, then remove the square representing the sound you omitted. You can put the picture of the stimulus word on the board.

Cake. (___ake) (Put 3 squares of different colors up. Remove the first one when you clap.) Response: /k/

Mice. (Mi___) Response: /s/

Listen for initial sounds

Activity:

Materials: Letter cards

> Teacher: Place the letter representing the targeted sound on the board. Tell the children you will say some words. When they hear the targeted sound at the beginning of the word, they are to clap their hands. Mix words with and without initial targeted sound in each grouping. Use vocabulary lists below.

Targeted sound is /k/.

Cake. Response: clap.
Eggs. Response: none.
Candy. Response: clap.

Other words to use:
Initial /k/ sound: cake, candy, can, cape, cup, corn
Initial /g/ sound: grape, ghost, goose,
Initial /b/ sound: beans, bowl, bread, bed

Omit the initial sound in a word containing only two or three sounds

Activity:

Materials: Felt squares of colored blocks – optional

> Instructions: Explain to the children that you want them to leave out the first sound in some words. Use only words containing 2 or three sounds. Place the same number of squares on the board as sounds represented. Remove the first colored square as the children say the last sounds(s).

Say leg. Response: leg.
Teacher: Now say leg without the /l/. Response: egg.
Say bed. Response: bed.
Teacher: Now say bed without /b/. Response: Ed.

Add an initial sound

Activity:

Materials: One- and two-syllable words from vocabulary list

> Instructions: Explain that you will say a sound or part of a word and the children are to change the word by adding a sound to the beginning.

Say ice. Response: ice.
Teacher: Now say it with /m/ at the beginning. Response: mice.

Other words: ice to rice, egg to leg, an to pan, an to can, Ed to bed.

Substitute an initial sound

Activity:

Materials: Vocabulary list

> Instructions: Explain that you will say a word and the children are to change the first sound to make a new word.

Say leg. Response: leg.
Teacher: Now say it but use the sound /b/ in place of /l/. Response: beg.
Teacher: Say goose. Response: goose.
Teacher: Now say it but use /m/ in place of the /g/. Response: moose.

Listen for the final sounds /k, t, s/

Activity:

Materials: None

> Instructions: I will say some words. When you hear the targeted sound at the end of the word, say the sound. Mix words with and without final targeted sound in each grouping. Use vocabulary list. To begin sound-symbol association put the letter representing the sound on the board.

Targeted final sound /k/:
    Cake. Response: /k/.
    Ghost. Response: none.
    Bake. Response: /k/.
    Corn. Response: /k/.

Targeted final sound /t/:
    Beet. Response: /t/.
    Meat. Response: /t/
    Bake. Response: none.
    Feet. Response: /t/.

Targeted final sound /s/:
    Ice. Response: /s/.
    Mice. Response: /s/
    Cake. Response: none.
    Rice. Response: /s/.

Omit the final sound in a word

Activity:

Materials: Pictures – optional
           Felt squares

> Instructions: Explain that you want them to leave out the last sound in some words. Use only words containing 4 or less sounds. Use squares representing each sound. When the children respond, remove the last felt representing the sound omitted. You can also talk about the number of sounds during this activity.

Say bean. Response: bean.
Teacher: Now say bean without the /n/. Response: bee.

Other words:
Goose to goo
Moose to moo
Ice to I
Rice to rye
Peach to pea
Grape to gray

Add the final sound

Activity:

Materials: Vocabulary list
            Ball

> Instructions: Instructions: Tell the children you will tell them a sound. Then you will say part of a word and they are to finish the word with their sound when you roll a ball to them.

Say goo.
Response: Goo.
Teacher: Now say it with /s/ at the end.
Response: Goose.

Other words to use:
Bee to bean
Moo to moose
I to ice
Rye to rice
Pea to Peach
Gray to grape

Substitute the final sound

Activity:

Materials: Vocabulary list

> Instructions: Explain that you will say a word and the children are to change the last sound to a different sound to make a new word.

Teacher: Say bed. Response: bed.
Teacher: Now say bed but use the sound /h/ in place of /b/. Response: head.
Teacher: Say cake. Response: cake.
Teacher: Now say it but use /l/ in place of the /k/. Response: lake.

Corn to horn
Horn to corn
Cheese to keys
Keys to cheese
Moose to juice
Juice to moose

Onset-rhyme

Activity:

Materials: None

> Instructions: Tell the children you will tell them two words and they are to tell you if the words rhyme.

Teacher: Do these words rhyme?

Cake – bed. Response: no.
Moose – goose. Response: yes.
Juice – grape. Response: no.
Cheese – keys. Response: yes.

Blend sounds to create words

Activity:

Materials: None

> Instructions: Tell the children you will speak like a robot and they are to guess what you said. Speak with a short pause between each sound. If this is an easy task for the students, make the pauses longer or choose longer words.

J – ui – ce. Response: juice.
Gh – o – s – t. Response: ghost.
Ch – ee – se Response: cheese.
S – n – a – ke. Response: snake.

ROCKS IN MY SOCKS AND RAINBOWS TOO

ACTIVITIES

Materials

Materials:
- Thunder tube – can be purchased through Children's Publishing
- Flashlight
- Reproducible pictures – included
- Rainstick – see instructions for making
- Clay for making rocks – can be purchased at hobby store
- Paint for coloring rocks
- Reproducible pictures – included
- Rocks collected from outside if you live in an area with rocks or rocks purchased from a landscaper
- Pan or pail to drop rocks in for sound effects

Vocabulary Familiarization Activity

1. Do a unit on senses. Talk about thunder storms but in a cautious manner so as not to frighten children who may be fearful of thunder. If possible, darken the room a little and show lightning with a flashlight. Use the thunder tube to talk about hearing thunder before the lightning comes. Make clouds with cotton balls glued on paper.

> Hear: Thunder – thunder tube. Hear rain.
> See: Lightning – flashlight (Darken the room a little to simulate clouds darkening.)
> Feel: Rain – Have the students sit in a circle with closed eyes. Let them know you will put droplets of water on their heads so they can feel the rain.
> Feel: Wind – use a fan to simulate the wind.

2. Color activities:

Cut out two socks with construction paper. Glue them together around edges to allow for putting rocks in them. Or, have the children bring in old socks. Make rocks out of clay and paint them. Or, cut strips of construction paper and allow the children to wad them for pretend rocks.

Color a picture of a sun. Make rainbows with the colored rocks. This is a good activity for matching colors and talking about same and different.

3. Have a treasure hunt for rocks. See if the children can find different colors. While reading the story allow the children to put the colored rocks (or M&M's) in their socks as Corey says the color he likes.

Vocabulary List

rocks	socks	fox
box	blocks	clock
blue	red	yellow
green	white	purple
pink	black	orange
gray	gold	sun
sunshine	tree	moo
raincloud	rainstorm	raindrop
rain	rainbow	sink
sack	rumble	goose
moose	big	bigger
biggest	small	smaller
smallest	Mommy	Corey
lightning	wagon	

Vocabulary by Sound

/r/ Initial: rocks, red, rain, rain cloud, raindrop, rainbow, rumble
   Medial: orange

/s/ Initial: socks, small, smaller, smallest, sun
   Final: socks, fox, blocks, box, goose, moose

/b/ Initial: box, blocks, blue, black, big, bigger, biggest
   Medial: rumble

/g/ Initial: green, gray
   Medial: bigger, biggest
   Final: big

Animal/Environmental Sound Awareness Activities

Locate the sounds

Activity:

Materials: Thunder tube
Flashlight

Instructions: Have an assistant go to another part of the room while the children close their eyes. The assistant will shake the thunder tube. (Caution: It is best that the children do not shake it without close supervision as the spring may accidentally hurt the child.) The children will open their eyes and tell where the thunder was.

Same/different sounds

Activity:

Materials: Rocks and pail or pan
Thunder tube

Instructions: Tell the children that you will make two sounds behind a screen and they are to tell you if they are same or different. Present the sounds several times.

Count the sounds

Activity:

Materials: Rocks (up to ten)
Pail or pan

Instructions: Tell the children you will allow one child at a time to drop rocks in the pail while the others close their eyes and count. Allow all the children an opportunity to place rocks in the pail. Ask the children how many times they heard rock sounds they heard.

Word Awareness Activities

Count the words

Activity:

> Instructions: Tell the children you will say a sentence and they are to tell you how many words you said.

Teacher: I will say a sentence and you tell me how many words I said.

> Rain, run! (2)
> I hear thunder. (3)
> Play with blocks. (3)
> Big, bigger, biggest! (3)
> I like gold rocks. (4)
> I have rocks in my socks. (5)

Listen for words

Activity:

Materials: None

> Instructions: Tell the children that you will say a sentence with a color. When they hear a color they are to pretend to color in the air.

> I like blue. Response: Color in air.
> I like to play. No response.
> The sky is blue. Response: Color in air.
> The rock is pink. Response: Color in air.
> Give me a gold rock. Response: Color in air.
> The cloud is big. No response.

Listen for same or different words

Activity:

Materials: Pictures – optional

> Instructions: Tell the children that you will say some words and they are to tell you if they are same or different.

>Pink, pink. Response: same.
>Rocks, rain. Response: different.
>Blue, blue. Response: same.
>Mommy, mommy. Response: same.
>Rain, thunder. Response: different.

Listen for missing words in a sequence of words

Activity:

Materials: Pictures of colors – optional
            Felt Squares – optional

> Instructions: Tell the children you will say some words. They you will say them again and they are to tell you which word you forgot to say. In the beginning it is best to use pictures. Put the pictures on a felt board. Remove the pictures as you say the words. Then put up the pictures in the same order but with one missing. The students should tell you the missing picture. When the children are familiar with the activity, eliminate the use of the pictures and use felt squares or only say the words.

>Blue, pink, gray. Blue, ____, gray. Response: pink.
>Rain, thunder, sock. ____, thunder, sock. Response: rain.
>Blocks, red, thunder, blue. Blocks, red, _____, blue. Response: thunder.

Listen for missing words in a sentence

Activity:

Materials: None

> Instructions: Tell the children you will say a sentence two times. The second time you say it you will forget a word and they are to help you by telling you what word you left out. This can also be done during the reading of the repetitive passages. Occasionally, pause and let the children finish the sentence.

>I have rocks in my socks. I have rocks in my _____. Response: socks.
>Play with your blocks. Play with your _____. Response: blocks.
>Your sock grew. Your sock _____. Response: grew.
>Ooh, I like blue rocks. Ooh, I like blue _____. Response: rocks.
>We'll be home soon. We'll be home _____. Response: soon.
>I see rain clouds. I see _____. Response: rain clouds.

Listen for a different word out of a 3-word sequence

Activity:

Materials: None

> Instructions: Tell the children you will say three words. One word will be different. They are to tell you the word that is different.

    Blue, red, blue. Response: red
    Gray, gray, pink. Response: pink
    Rain, thunder, thunder. Response: rain
    Rock, rock, lightning. Response: lightning

Blend words to create compound word

Activity:

Materials: Pictures – raindrop, rain cloud, rainbow

> Instructions: Tell the children you will try to trick them by saying words slow in your robotic voice. They are to guess the word. Put pictures of similar compound words on the felt board. Say the word with a pause between; i.e., rain-pause-cloud. This helps the students listen for the remainder of the word while becoming aware of using parts to create new words.

    Rain (pause) bow. Response: Rainbow
    Rain (pause) drop. Response: Raindrop
    Rain (pause) cloud. Response: Rain cloud

Syllable Awareness Activities

Count the syllables

Activity:

Materials: Vocabulary list
   Mirror – optional
   M & M's (CAUTION: BE CAREFUL OF ANY WHO HAVE ALLERGIES TO PEANUTS!)

> Instructions: Tell the children you will say a word and they are to tell you how many syllables (how many times their chin moves) are in the word.

   Lightning (2)
   Rocks (1)
   Corey (2)
   Rumble (2)
   Thunderstorm (3)
   Blue (1)

Delete a syllable

Activity:

Materials: Pictures – optional
   Vocabulary list

> Instructions: Tell the children that you will say a word. Then they say the word with part missing.

   Say Mommy. Response: Mommy. Now say it without -my. Response: Mo.
   Say Mommy. Response: Mommy. Now say it without Mo-. Response: -my.

   Thunder without der. Response: thun.
   Thunder without thun. Response: der.
   Biggest without bi. Response: gest.
   Biggest without gest. Response: bi or big is acceptable.
   Lightning without light. Response: ning.
   Lightning without ning. Response: light.

Add a missing syllable

Activity:

Materials: Pictures
          Mirror

> Instructions: Explain that you will say a part of a word and the children are to guess what the word is. Once the children are familiar with the words you use, discontinue using the pictures. On this you can roll a ball as you say the first syllable(s) and the child to whom the ball is rolled will say the last syllable.

Finish these words for me:
    Thun(der), light(ning), Mom(my), Co(rey), wa(gon)

Blend syllables to create words

Activity:

Materials: Pictures – optional
          Vocabulary list

> Instructions: Tell the children you will say some syllables in a robotic voice and they are to guess the word.

    Mom (pause) my. Response: Mommy.
    Light (pause) ning. Response: lightning.
    Wa (pause) gon. Response: wagon.
    Big (pause) ger. Response: bigger.
    Big (pause) gest. Response: biggest.
    Co (pause) rey. Response: Corey.
    Thun (pause) der. Response: thunder.

Speech Sound Awareness

Count the sounds

Activity:

Materials: Pictures initially or felt squares

Instructions: Tell the children you will say some sounds and they are to tell how many were said. Use manipulatives and physical movements; i.e. clapping. If necessary, drop rocks in a pail and count them after the response. If you use felt squares, place a square for each sound and make them different colors for different sounds.

B – l – ue. 3 squares of different colors
R – e – d. 3 squares of different colors
R – o – ck – s. 4 squares of different colors
S – o – ck – s. 4 squares with square 1 and 4 the same representing /s/

Listen for same or different initial sounds

Activity:

Materials: Vocabulary list

Instructions: Tell the children you will say two words. They are to tell if the first sound in the words is same or different.

Fox-goose. Response: different.   Sack-sock. Response: same.
Green-gray. Response: same.   Small-sock. Response: same.
Box-rain. Response: different.   Sun-Corey. Response: different.

Listen for missing sounds

Activity:

Materials: Felt squares
          Vocabulary list

> Instructions: Tell the children you will say a word two times. The second time you will leave out a sound and they are to tell the missing sound. Remember to give the sound and not the letter. If you use the felt squares place the same number of squares as sounds on the board. First, say the word, then remove the square representing the sound you omitted.

Teacher: Shoe. ___ – oo. (2 squares of different colors, remove the first one and you say /oo/) Response: /sh/.
Teacher: Goose. ___ – oose. Response: /g/.
Teacher: Rain. Rai___. Response: /n/.

Listen for initial sounds

Activity:

Materials: Letter cards

> Instructions: Place the letter representing the targeted sound on the board. Tell the children you will say some words. When they hear the targeted sound at the beginning of the word, they are to say the targeted sound. Mix words with and without initial targeted sound in each grouping. Use vocabulary lists at beginning of this chapter.

Targeted sound /b/:

Box. Response: /b/.
Rain. Response: none.
Block. Response: /b/.

Other target sounds – /s/, /g/

Omit the initial sound in a word containing only two or three sounds

Activity:

Materials: Felt squares – optional

> Instructions: Explain to the children that you want them to leave out the first sound in some words. Place the same number of squares on the board as sounds represented. Remove the first colored square as the children say the last sounds(s).

Say gray. Response: Gray.
Teacher: Now say gray without the /g/. Response: /ray/.

Additional stimulus words:
Red without /r/. Response ed.
Sink without /s/. Response ink.
Gold without /g/. Response old.
Blue without /b/. Response lue.

Add an initial sound

Activity:

Materials: One-syllable words from Vocabulary list

> Instructions: Explain that you will say a sound or part of a word and the children are to make a new word by adding a sound to the beginning.

Teacher: Say ox. Response: ox.
Teacher: Now say it with /b/ at the beginning. Response: box.

Additional stimulus words:

Add /g/ to old.
Add /s/ to ink.
Add /g/ to ray.
Add /b/ to lock.
Add /b/ to lue.
Add /f/ to ox.
Add /r/ to ox.

Substitute an initial sound

Activity:

Materials: Vocabulary list

> Instructions: Explain that you will say a word and the children are to change the first sound to make a new word.

Say box. Response: box.
Now say it but use the sound /f/ in place of /b/. Response: fox.

Additional stimulus words:

Fox to locks
Locks to rocks
Block to clock
Rain to cane
Rain to mane
Rain to lane

Listen for final sound

Activity:

Materials: None

> Instructions: I will say some words. When you hear the targeted sound at the end of the word, say the sound. Mix words with and without final targeted sound in each grouping. Use vocabulary list.

Targeted final sound /s/:

    Goose. Response: /s/.
    Tree. Response: none.
    Fox. Response: /s/.
    Moose. Response: /s/.
    White. Response: none.
    Rocks. Response: /s/.
    Wagon. Response: none.

Additional final sounds:
/k/ black, clock, sack
/n/ green, rain, sun

Omit the final sound in a word

Activity:

Materials: Pictures – optional
            Felt squares – optional

> Instructions: Tell the children that you want them to leave out the last sound in some words. Use only words containing 4 or less sounds. When the children respond, remove the last felt representing the sound omitted. You can also talk about the number of sounds during this activity.

Say rain. Response: rain.
Now say rain without the /n/. Response: ray.
Say white. Response: white.
Now say white without the /t/. Response: why.

Additional stimulus words:

Moose – moo
Goose – goo
Rock – rah

Add a final sound

Activity:

Materials: None

> Instructions: Tell the children you will tell them a sound. Then you will say part of a word and they are to finish the word with their sound when you roll a ball to them.

Teacher: Say ray. Response: ray.
Teacher: Now say it with /n/ at the end. Response: rain.

Additional stimulus words:

Why – white
Moo – moose
Goo – goose
Rah – rock

Substitute a final sound

Activity:

Materials: Vocabulary list

> Instructions: Explain that you will say a word and the children are to change the last sound to a different sound to make a new word.

Teacher: Say green. Response: green.
Teacher: Now say green but use the sound /t/ in place of /n/. Response: greet.

Additional stimulus words:

Tree – tray.
Gray – grape.
Blue – blow.
Sack – sad.
Sack – sat.
Rain – raid.
Clock – clod.

Onset-rhyme

Activity:

Materials: None

Instructions:

Teacher: Do these words rhyme?

> Rain – rock. Response: No.
> Shoe – grew. Response: Yes.
> Fox – box. Response: Yes.
> Big – sun. Response: No.
> Blue – shoe. Response: Yes.
> Rocks – socks. Response: Yes.

Blend sounds to create words

Activity:

Materials: None

> Instructions: I will speak like a robot and you guess what I am saying. (Speak with a short pause between each sound. If this is an easy task for the students, make the pauses longer or choose longer words.)

    R – ai – n. Response: rain.
    G – oo – se. Response: goose.
    S – o – ck. Response: sock.
    B – i – g. Response: big.

Additional stimulus words are in Vocabulary list.

THE FROG WHO COULD NOT CROAK

ACTIVITIES

Materials

A. Exercises
B. Animal masks – reproducible
C. Small reproducible pictures of animals – reproducible
D. Instructions for student-made rainstick, student-made flies

    1. Student-made rainstick: Using a long wrapping paper tube, hammer drywall nails into the tube randomly. Fill it with about ½ cup rice. Seal the end of the tube with paper (fairly heavy-weight paper works best) taped on with masking tape. The tube can be decorated with tissue paper glued to the tube.

    2. Student-made flies: Use one pipe cleaners and colored tissue paper. Fold the pipe cleaner once. Twist the two ends around each other except for a quarter inch on one end. Allow this end to serve as the two antennae. Cut oval or rectangular strips of the tissue paper and twist the pipe cleaner around the center with the two ends protruding on the top for the antennae.

E. Optional purchases:
    (Contact Children's Publishing for ordering information.)
    Toucan puppet
    Wooden frog with rasp (creates true frog sound)
    Wooden cricket with rasp (creates true cricket sound)
    Thunder tube

Vocabulary Familiarization Activity

1. Color and cut out the large frog. Glue it to a larger piece of paper. Allow the children to draw a long tongue on the frog. Cut out small flies and let the children put flies on the sticky (glue) tongue. Each child can then count the flies on their frog's tongue. Or, allow the children to put the flies on the tongue as the frog catches a fly.

2. Make finger puppets with the reproducible pictures. The rainforest pictures can also be used for the bog scene. After the children become familiar with the dialogue allow them to put on a skit. Each child will repeat the dialogue when their animal appears in the story. One child can hold up a sign that says, "I am a green and gray striped frog who cannot croak. I do not know why I cannot croak." When the animal asks the frog why he cannot croak, that child will hold up the sign and the children in the audience will read it.

3. Have some children color the frog masks and the others color the toucan. Glue the popsicle sticks to the back. Play the CD from the kit. When the toucan sound comes up, the children with the toucan will hold up their masks. When the frog sound comes up, the children with the frog will hold up their masks.

Talk about frog's habitat. Use a lot of rhyming words when talking about the habitat; i.e. bog, fog, muck, mud, mucky, yucky, etc. Different frogs live in different places. Bring in pictures of different frogs and talk about the differences. There are many colorful frogs that live in the rainforest and you can download these pictures from the internet.

Vocabulary List

Frog	Bog	Fog
Dog	Dugger	Lolling
Green	Gray	Striped
Croak	Higgie	Hog
Fox	Fox	Moe
Crow	Yak	Backpack
Back	Goat	Rowboat
Rowing	Crocodile	Smile
Spunky	Monkey	Cape
Baboon	Tune	Mrs. Trog
Flies	Leaves	Rocks
Water	Rain	Raindrop
Tongue	One	Two
Three	Four	Five
Six	Seven	Eight
Nine	Ten	

Vocabulary by Sound

/b/ Initial: baboon, bog, back, baa, buzz
   Medial: baboon

/d/ Initial: dog, Dugger

/g/ Initial: goat, gray, green, grunt
   Medial: Dugger, Higgie
   Final: frog, bog, fog, dog, hog

/f/ Initial: frog, fog, fox, flies, four, five

/k/ Initial: crow, croak, crocodile, caw
   Medial: spunky, monkey, crocodile, sticky
   Final: croak, yak, back, oink, sack

/l/ Initial: log, lolling, leaves
   Medial: lolling
   Final: smile

/s/ Initial: smile, striped, sticky, spunky, six, seven

/t/ Initial: two, ten, tongue
   Final: eight

/th/ Initial: three

/m/ Initial: Moe, monkey

/n/ Initial: nine
   Final: ten, nine, rain, seven

/r/ Initial: rowboat, rowing, row, rocks

/r/ Blends: frog, green, gray, striped, croak, crow, grunt

Animal/Environmental Sound Awareness Activities

Find the sound

Activity:

Materials: Reproducible masks

> Instructions: Have one student take an animal/person picture from the box. Tell the other students to close their eyes while the student with the picture hides and then makes the sound of the animal/person represented by the picture. The other students can open their eyes and then tell where the animal/person is located.
>
> Variation: Have the students use noise toys; i.e., wooden croaking frog, wooden chirping cricket.

Locate the sounds

Activity:

Materials: Reproducible pictures of animals and persons

> Instructions: Divide the class in half. One half is given one picture from one stack. Have this half stand on one side of the room. The other half is given one picture from the other stack. They stand on the opposite side of the room. Number one group listens while number group two make the sounds of their animal/person. (It is best to allow one student at a time to make a sound. However, when the students are familiar with the game, you can then increase the level of difficulty by allowing two or three students to make their sound at the same time.) Group one students will then go to the person making the sound of his/her picture. Alternate and allow group two to listen while group one makes the sounds.

Identify the sounds

Activity:

Materials: Wooden frog noisemaker
Wooden cricket noisemaker
Rainstick

> Instructions: Have one student stand behind screen and make one noise with any of the above noisemakers. The other students then guess what it is. If you are using the frog and cricket, it will be necessary to practice because differentiating between the two may be difficult depending on the age.

Identify the sounds and their position left to right

Activity:

Materials: Small pictures of animals and persons

> Instructions: Have three students stand in front of class. Standing students take a picture card but do not show it to seated students. Tell the children to say their sounds when you tap them. The sounds will be presented to the seated students in a left-to-right progression (from their perspective). Ask the children what sound did they hear at the beginning, in the middle, at the end?

Same/different sounds

Activity:

Materials: Pictures

> Instructions: Have two students come to the front. Give each a picture, sometimes the same pictures and sometimes different pictures. Have each student say the animal sound. Ask the seated students if the sound is same or different.

Count the animal/person sounds

Activity:

Materials: Pictures of animals and sometimes a blank card

> Instructions: Have four students come to the front in a line. Give each one a paper with an animal picture or a blank card. Tap the students' shoulders left-to-right again. The students say his/her animal sound but the student(s) with blank card(s) says nothing. There may be times when one student is not tapped and, therefore, does not make a sound. At that point explain that only two sounds were heard but three animals were seen. Ask how many sounds did you hear?

Word Awareness Activities

Count the words

Activity:

Materials: Blocks or felt squares – optional

> Instructions: Tell the children you will say a sentence and they are to tell you the number of words said. Initially, it is good to use manipulatives, i.e., blocks, felt squares, etc., and/or physical movements; i.e. clapping, hopping, stepping on squares, etc. If necessary, pause between the words until the students understand the concept. When listening for the number of words in sentences it may be necessary for you to give longer pauses between words. This can be done easily during the reading of the story once the children are familiar with the dialogue.

    Good morning. (2)
    I cannot croak. (3)
    The frog said nothing. (4)
    The baboon is singing. (4)
    Let me count those flies. (5)

Listen for words

Activity:

Materials: None

> Instructions: Tell the children that you will hold up a picture of an animal and the animal will make a sound. If the animal says his sound correctly, they are to clap. If the animal says the wrong sound they are to tell the animal what to say.

    A dog says oink. Response: no, woof-woof (or bark).
    A monkey says "eee." Response: yes.
    A hog says oink. Response: yes.
    A yak says grunt. Response: yes.
    A crow says caw-caw. Response: yes.
    A fox says caw-caw. Response: no, yip, yip.
    A frog says croak. Response: yes.
    A dog says woof-woof. Response: yes.

Listen for words

Activity:

Materials: Animal list and sounds

> Instructions: Tell the children that you will say some words. When they hear the name of an animal, they are to make the sound of that animal.

    Dog. Response: woof-woof.
    Fox. Response: yip-yip.

Use additional stimulus words from list.

Listen for same or different words

Activity:

Materials: Vocabulary list
          Pictures – optional

> Instructions: Tell the children that you will say some words and they are to tell you if they are same or different.

    Frog, frog. Response: same
    Dog, fox. Response: different

Use additional words from list.

Listen for missing words in a sequence of words

Activity:

Materials: Pictures of animals
          Felt Squares
          Vocabulary list

> Instructions: Tell the children you will say some words. You will then repeat them but will forget one word. They are to tell the forgotten. In the beginning it is best to use pictures. Put the pictures on a felt board. Remove the pictures as you say the words. Then put up the pictures in the same order but with one missing. The students should tell you the missing picture. When the children are familiar with the activity, eliminate the use of the pictures use felt squares or only say the words.

    Goat, yak, monkey. Goat, (____), monkey. Response: yak.
    Crow, dog, baboon. (____), dog, baboon. Response: crow.
    Yak, goat, cricket. Yak, (____), ghost. Response: goat.
    Dog, yak, frog. (____), yak, frog. Response: dog.

Listen for missing words in a sentence

Activity:

Materials: None

> Instructions: Tell the children you will say a sentence two times and they are to help you by telling you what word you left out the second time. This can also be done during the reading of the repetitive passages. Occasionally, pause and let the children finish the sentence.

    A yak can grunt. A yak can (_____). Response: grunt.
    The frog said nothing. The frog said (_____). Response: nothing.
    The frog sat on a log. The (_____) sat on a log. Response: frog.
    The yak has a sack on his back. The yak has a sack on his (_____). Response: back.
    A baboon sings a tune. A baboon sings a (_____). Response: tune.
    The dog went for a walk. The dog went for a (_____). Response: walk.

Listen for a different word out of a 3-word sequence

Activity:

Materials: Vocabulary list

> Instructions: Tell the children you will say three words. They are to tell you the word that is different.

    Dog, fox, dog. Response: fox
    Log, tree, tree. Response: log

Syllable Awareness Activities

Count the syllables

Activity:

Materials: Vocabulary list
Mirror if necessary
M & M's (CAUTION: BE CAREFUL OF ANY WHO HAVE ALLERGIES TO PEANUTS!)

> Instructions: Tell the children you will say a word and they are to tell you how many syllables (how many times their chin moves) are in the word.

Spunky (2)
Fox (1)
Crocodile (3)
Baboon (2)
Flies (1)
Monkey (2)

Delete a syllable

Activity:

Materials: Pictures – optional
Vocabulary list

> Instructions: Tell the children you will say a word. Then the children are to say it without one syllable.

Say baboon. Response: baboon. Now say it without ba. Response: boon.
Say baboon. Response: baboon. Now say it without boon. Response: ba.

Other stimulus words:
Crocodile without dile
Rowboat without boat
Rowboat without row
Sticky without y
Sticky without stick

Add a missing syllable

Activity:

Materials: Pictures
            Mirror
            Ball
            Vocabulary list (2-3 syllable words)

> Instructions: Display pictures of all stimulus items. Explain that you will say a part of a word and the children are to guess what the word is. Once the children are familiar with the words you use, discontinue using the pictures. On this you can roll a ball as you say the first syllable(s) and the child to whom the ball is rolled will say the last syllable.

I am thinking of something that says "eee-eee" and swings in a tree. It is a mon(___).
Response: key.
I am thinking of something that lives in water and is green. It is a croco(___).
Response: dile.

Blend syllables to create words

Activity:

Materials: Pictures – optional
            Vocabulary list

> Instructions: Tell the children you will say some syllables in a robotic voice and they are to guess the word.

    Mon (pause) key. Response: monkey
    Cro (pause) co (pause) dile. Response: crocodile

Speech Sound Awareness

Count the sounds

Activity:

Materials: Pictures – optional
　　　　　　Felt squares – optional
　　　　　　Vocabulary list

> Instructions: Tell the children you will say some sounds and they are to tell you how many you said. Use manipulatives and physical movements; i.e. clapping. If necessary, drop tokens in a box and count them after the response. If you use felt squares, place a square for each sound and make them different colors for different sounds.

　　　B – a – ck. 2 squares of different colors
　　　R – ow. 2 squares of different colors
　　　Y – a – k. 3 squares of different colors

Listen for same or different initial sounds

Activity:

Materials: Vocabulary list

> Instructions: Say two words. Tell if the first sound in the words is same or different.

　　　Crow – smile. Response: different.
　　　Baboon – baa. Response: same.
　　　Frog – fox. Response: same
　　　Log – back Response: different

Listen for missing sounds

Activity:

Materials: Felt squares
　　　　　　Vocabulary list

> Instructions: Tell the children you will say a word two times. The second time you will leave out a sound and they are to tell you what sound you forgot. Remember to give the sound and not the letter. If you use the felt squares place the same number of squares as sounds on the board. First, say the word, then remove the square representing the sound you omitted.

Teacher: Back. Ba – __. (3 squares of different colors, remove the last. Response /k/.
Teacher: Moc. M – __. Response: /oe/
Teacher: Goat. G – __ – t. Response: /oe/

Listen for initial sounds /g, k, b, s, f/

Activity:

Materials: Letter cards

> Teacher: Place the letter representing the targeted sound on the board. Tell the children you will say some words. When they hear the targeted sound at the beginning of the word, they are to say the sound. Mix words with and without initial targeted sound in each grouping.

Targeted sound /g/:

Goat. Response: /g/.
Tree. Response: none.
Green. Response: /g/.

Initial /k/ sound: crow, croak, crocodile, caw
Initial /b/ sound: baboon, bog, back, baa, buzz
Initial /s/ sound: smile, striped, sticky, spunky
Initial /f/ sound: frog, fog, fox, flies

Omit the initial sound in a word containing only two or three sounds

Activity:

Materials: Colored felt squares – optional
          Vocabulary list

> Instructions: Explain to the children that you want them to leave out the first sound in some words. Use only words containing 2 or three sounds. Place the same number of squares on the board as sounds represented. Remove the first colored square as the children say the last sounds(s).

Teacher: Say, goat. Response: goat.
Teacher: Now say goat without the /g/. Response: /oat/.
Teacher: Say fox. Response: fox.
Teacher: Now say fox without /f/. Response: /ox/.

Other stimulus words:
Crow without /k/
Caw without /k/
Smile without /s/
Sticky without /s/
Gray without /g/
Row without /r/

Add an initial sound

Activity:

Materials: Vocabulary list

> Instructions: Explain that you will say a sound or part of a word and the children are to change the word by adding a sound to the beginning.

Teacher: Say oat.
Response: Oat.
Teacher: Now say it with /g/ at the beginning.
Response: Goat.

Other stimulus words:

Ox with /f/
Row with /k/
Aw with /k/
Mile with /s/
Ray with /g/
Owe with /r/

Activity:

Materials: Vocabulary list

> Instructions: Tell the children you will play the monkey and baboon game. Explain that the monkey says "eee-eee" and the baboon says "ooo-ooo." The children are to help the monkey and the baboon speak in people language by adding people sounds (consonants) to the beginning of the monkey and baboon sounds.

    Bee-bee   Boo-boo
    Dee-dee   Moo-moo
    Fee-fee   Foo-foo

Continue adding consonants through the alphabet.

Substitute an initial sound

Activity:

Materials: Vocabulary list

> Instructions: Explain that you will say a word and the children are to change the first sound to make a new word.

Teacher: Say log. Response: log.
Teacher: Now say it but use the sound /b/ in place of /l/. Response: bog.
Teacher: Say dog. Response: dog.
Teacher: Now say it but use /h/ in place of the /d/. Response: hog.

Other stimulus words:
Goat to boat
Gray to tray
Back to sack
Back to bad
Sack to back
Sack to sad
Fox to box
Box to fox
Moe to row

Listen for final sounds /g, k/

Activity:

Materials: Vocabulary list

> Instructions: Put the letter representing the targeted sound on the board. Tell the children you will say some words. When they hear the targeted sound at the end of the word, they are to say that sound. Mix words with and without final targeted sound in each grouping. Use vocabulary list.

Targeted final sound /g/:

Log. Response: /g/.
Tree. Response: none.
Bag. Response: /g/.
Hog. Response: /g/.

Additional stimulus words:
/g/ dog, fog, frog
/k/ croak, yak, back, oink, sack

Omit the final sound in a word

Activity:

Materials: Pictures – optional
Felt squares – optional

> Instructions: Explain that you want the children to leave out the last sound in some words. Use only words containing 4 or less sounds. Use squares representing each sound. When the children respond, remove the last felt representing the sound omitted. You can also talk about the number of sounds during this activity.

Teacher: Say goat.
Response: Goat.
Teacher: Now say goat without the /t/.
Response: Go.

Croak to crow
Boat to bow
Sticky to stick
Grape to gray

Add the final sound

Activity:

Materials: Vocabulary list, ball

> Instructions: Put the stimulus word pictures on the board. Have the children sit in a circle. Say the word two times. The second time you will omit the final sound. The child to whom the ball is rolled is to say the new word.

Pictures – optional

Teacher: Say go.
Response: Go.
Teacher: Now say go with a /t/ at the end.
Response: Goat.

Crow to croak
Bow to boat
Stick to sticky
Gray to grape

Substitute a final sound

Activity:

Materials: Vocabulary list

> Instructions: Explain that you will say a word and the children are to change the last sound to a different sound to make a new word.

Teacher: Say green. Response: green.
Teacher: Now say green but use the sound /t/ in place of /n/. Response: greet.
Teacher: Say dog. Response: Dog.
Teacher: Now say it but use /k/ in place of the /g/. Response: Dock.

Horse – horn
Hoot – hoop
Bat – bad
Back – bat
Back – bag
Bat – bam
Boat – bowl
Baboon – baboose
Baboon – babool
Baboon – babook
Baboon – baboop

Onset-rhyme

Activity:

Materials: Vocabulary list

> Instructions: Tell the children to listen to two words. They are to tell you if the words rhyme?

    Hog – tree. Response: no.
    Dog – log. Response: yes.
    Back – yak. Response: yes.

Refer to vocabulary list for more stimulus words.

Blend sounds to create words

Activity:

Materials: None

> Instructions: Tell the children you will say a word in a robotic voice and they are to guess what the word is said. Speak with a short pause between each sound. If this is an easy task for the students, make the pauses longer or choose longer words.

    L – o – g. Response: log.
    S – a – ck. Response: sack.
    G – oa – t. Response: goat.

Refer to vocabulary list for more stimulus words.

REFERENCES & SUGGESTED READINGS

1. Culatta, B., D. Kovarsky, G. Theadore, A. Franklin, G. Timler. 2003. Quantitative and Qualitative Documentation of Early Literacy Instruction. *American Journal of Speech-Language Pathology*: Vol. 12, 172-188, May 2003.

2. Flege, J. E. (1991) The interlingual identification of Spanish and English vowels: Orthographic evidence. The Quarterly Journal of Experimental Psychology, 43A(3), 701-731.

3. Goldsworthy, C. (1996) *Developmental reading disabilities: A language-based treatment approach.* San Diego, CA: Singular Publishing.

4. International Dyslexia Association: www.interdys.org

5. Lindamood, Charles H., Lindamood, Particia C. (1969, 1975). Auditory Discrimination in Depth. Austin, TX: Pro-Ed.

6. Robertson, S., Davig, H. (2002). *Read With Me!.* Eau Claire, WI: Thinking Publications.

7. Texas EducationAssociation: http://www.tea.state.tx.us/curriculum/early/prekguide.html

8. Torgerson, J. K., R. K. Wagner, C. A. Rashotte, A. W. Alexander, and T. Conway, 1997. Preventative and remedial interventions for children with severe reading disabilities. Learning Disabilities: A Multi-Disciplinary Journal 8: 51-62.

9. Worden, P.E., & Boettcher, W. (1990). Young children's acquisition of alphabet knowledge. *Journal of Reading Behavior*, 22, 277-295.

REPRODUCIBLES

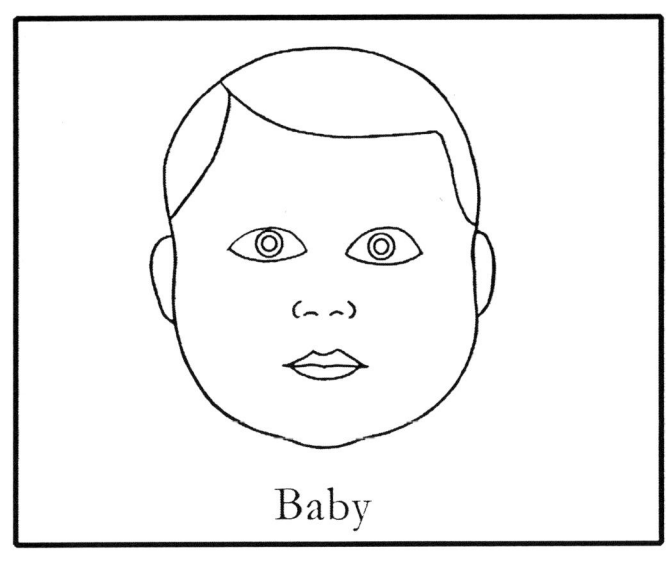
Baby

Baboon

Bat

Bear

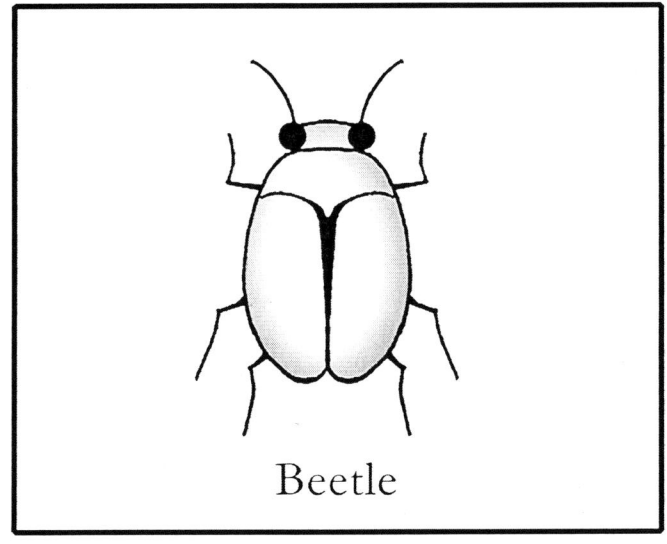
Beetle

Bird

Butterfly

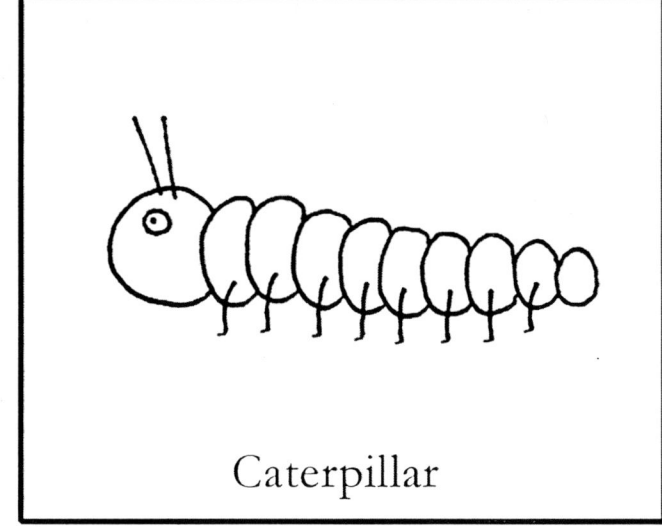
Caterpillar

Cow

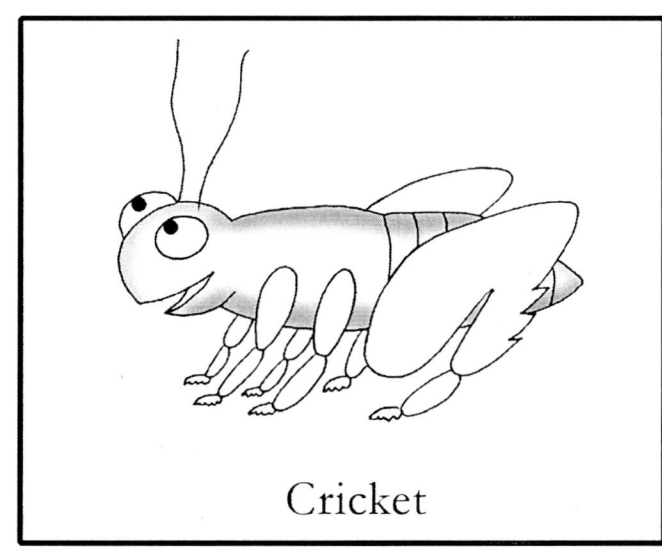
Cricket

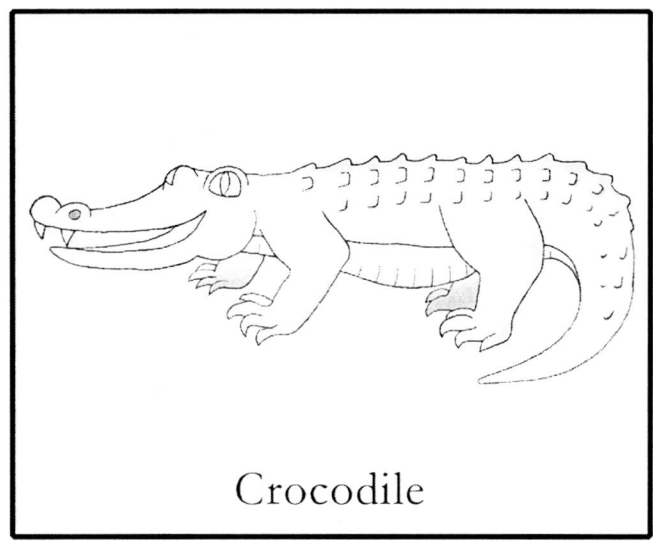
Crocodile

Crow

Dog

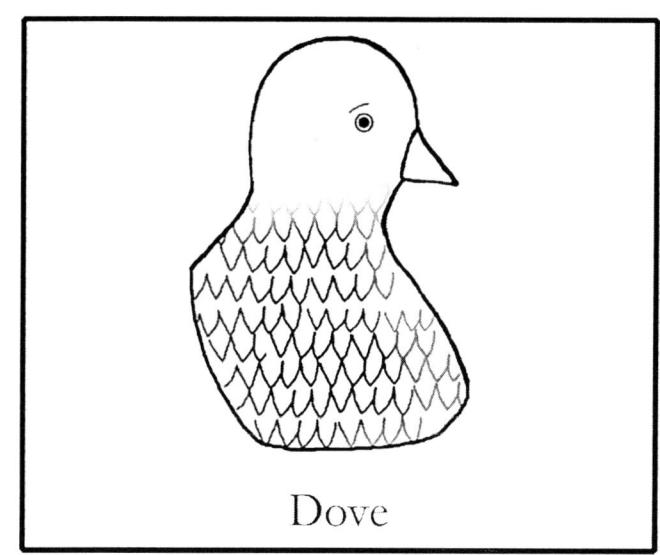
Dove

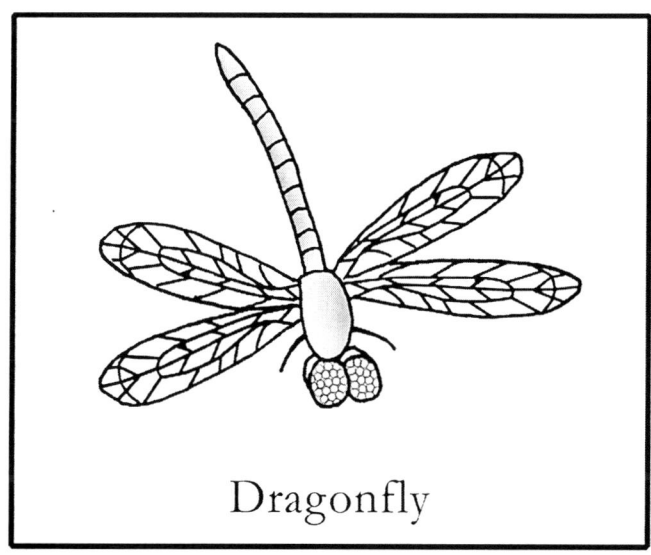
Dragonfly

Elephant

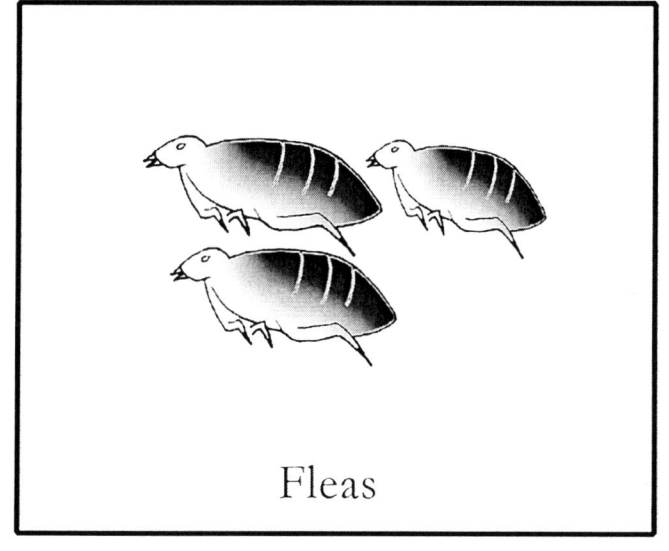
Fleas

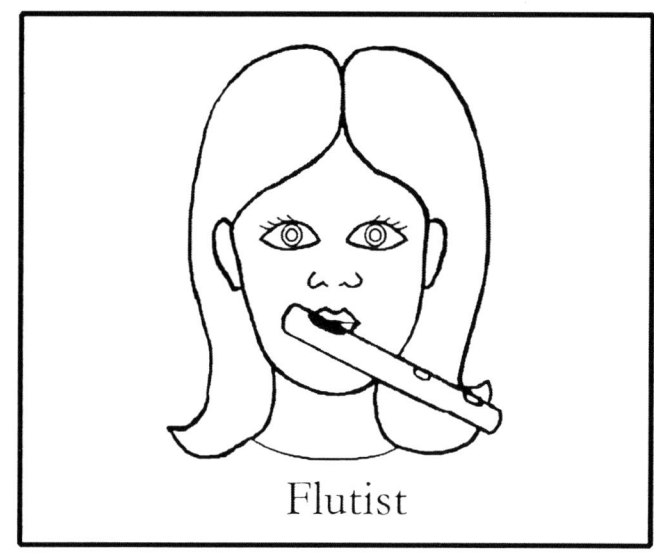
Flutist

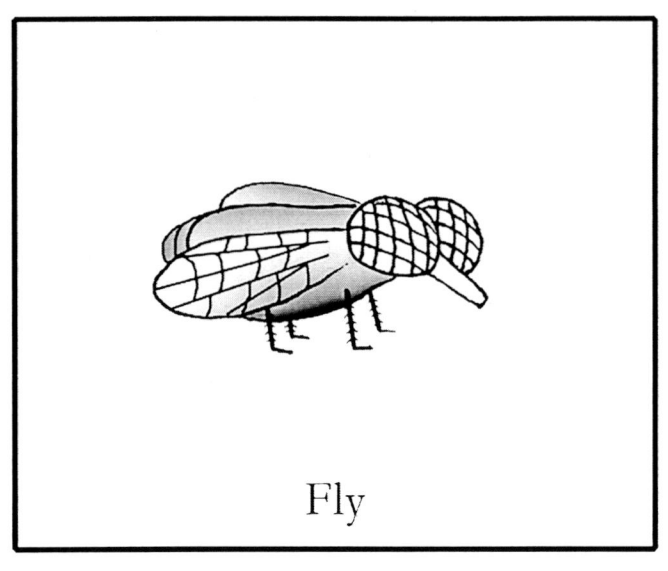
Fly

Fox

Frog

Gecko Lizard

Ghost

Goat

Goose

Gorilla

Hen

Hog (pig)

Horse

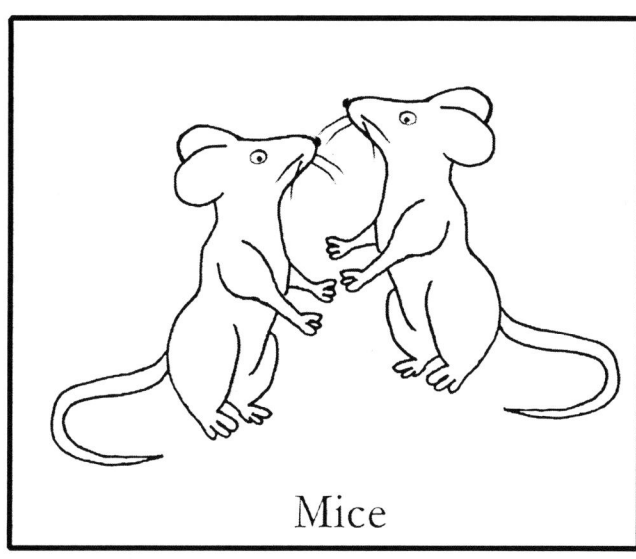
Mice

Monkey

Moose

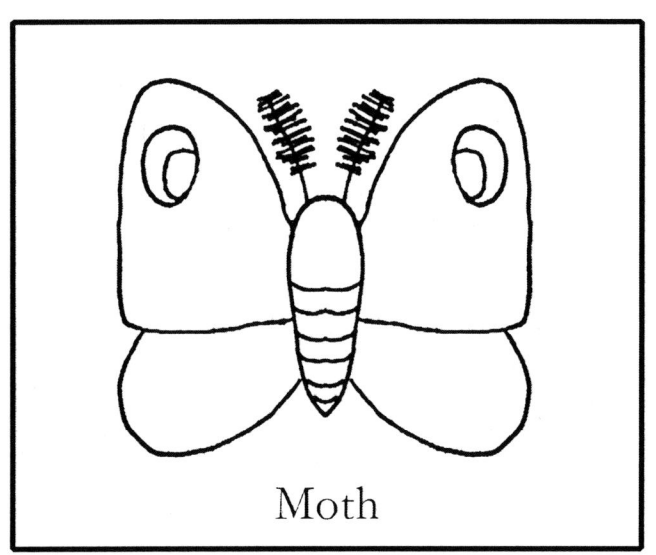
Moth

Owl

Road Runner

Snake

Toad

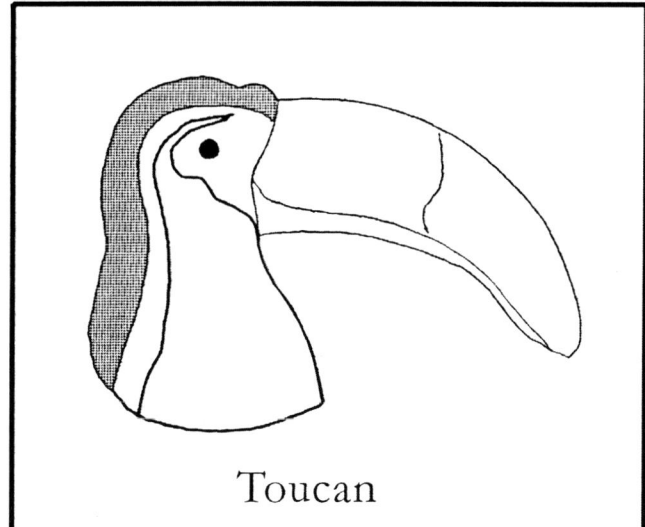
Toucan

Yak

Banana

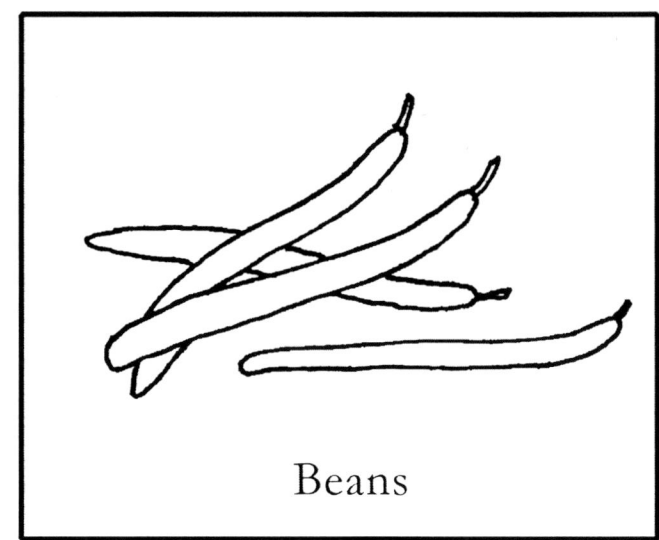
Beans

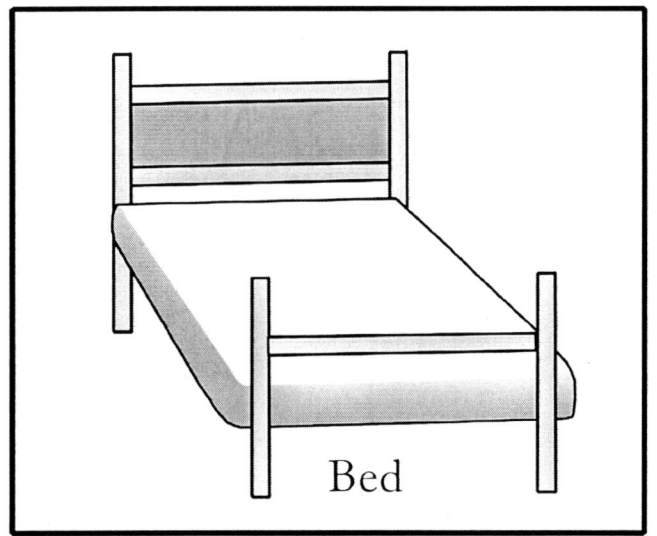
Bed

Blocks

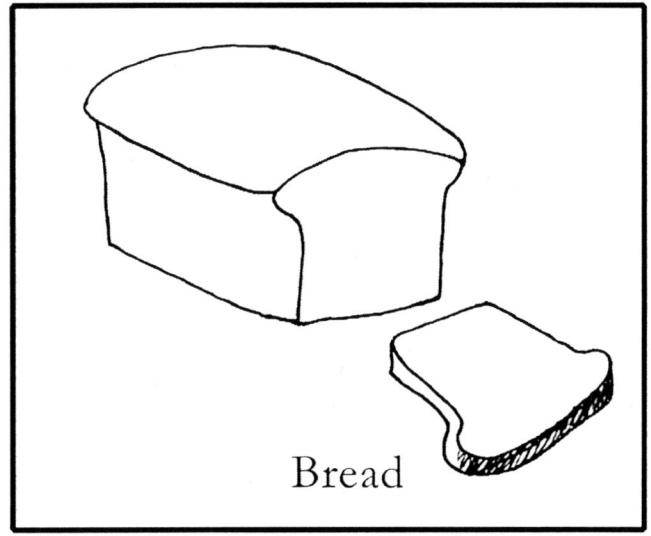
Bread

Cake

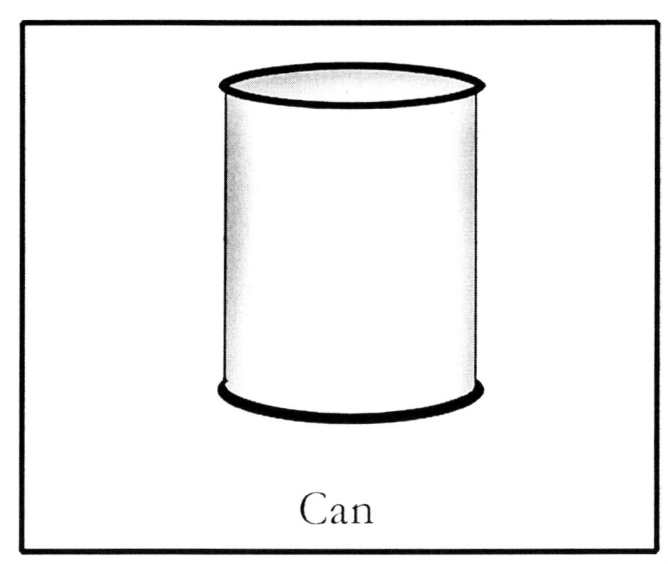
Can

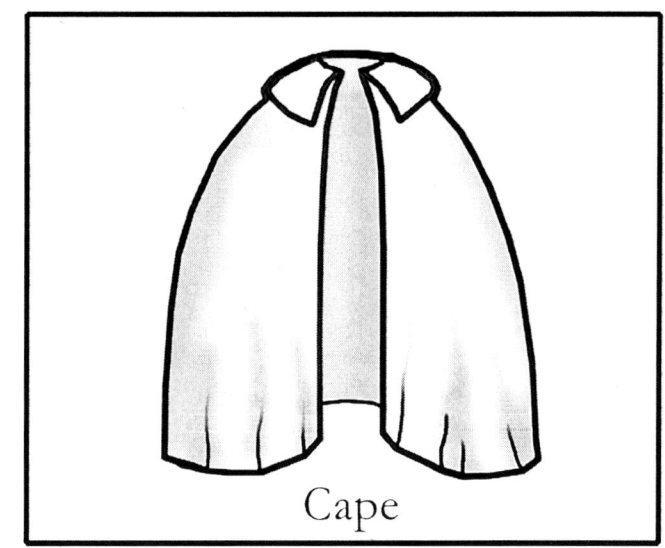
Cape

Cheese

Clock

Coconut

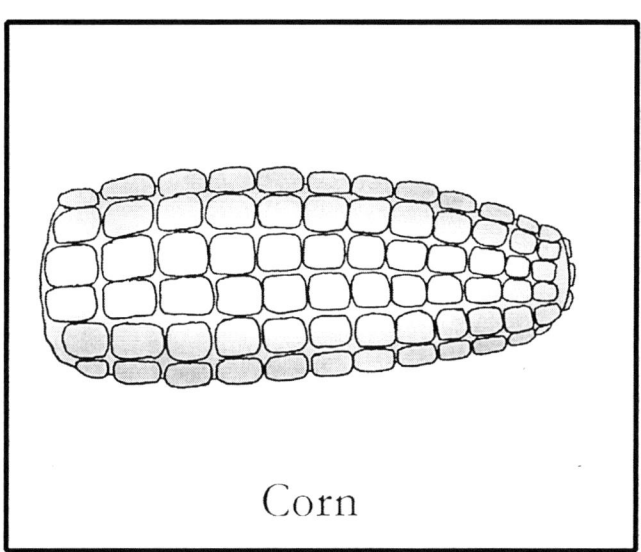
Corn

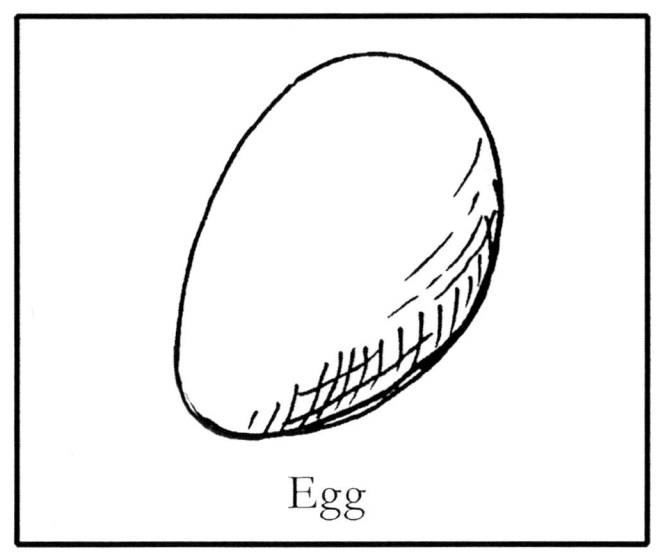
Egg

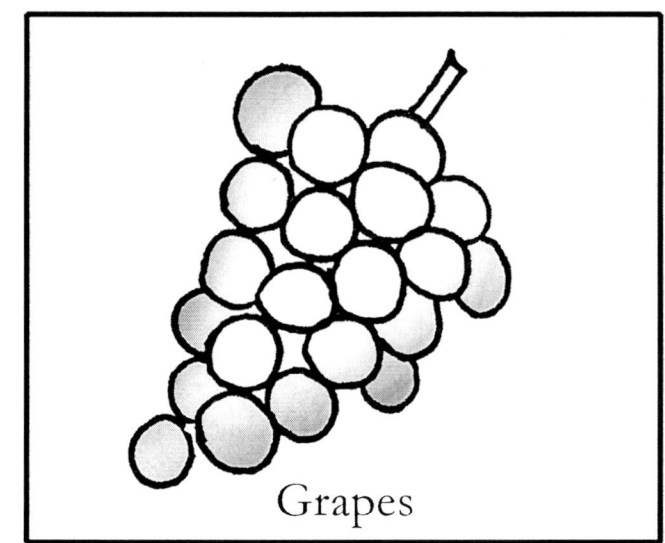
Grapes

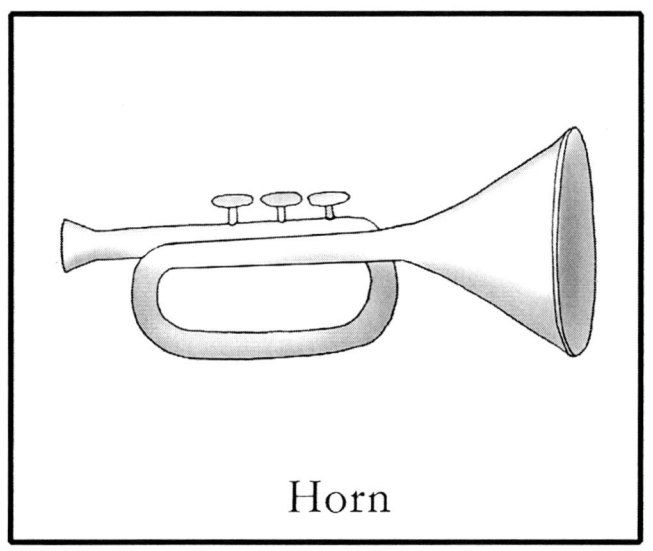
Horn

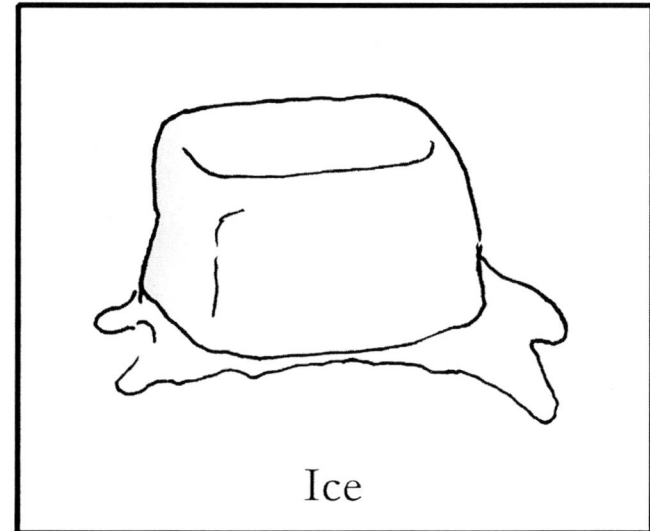
Ice

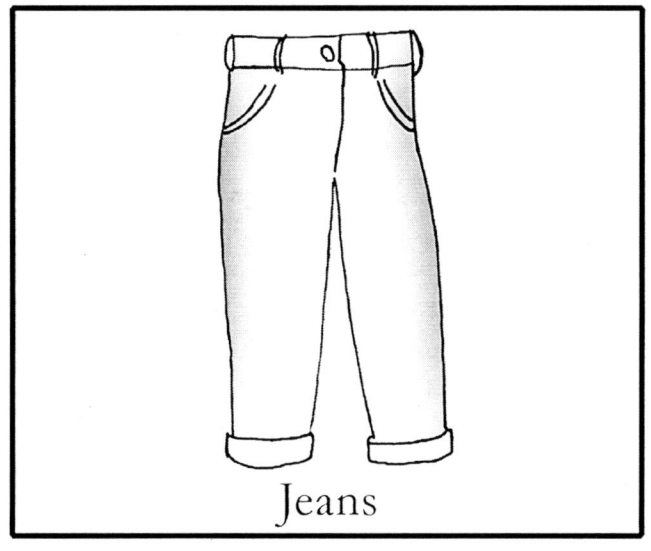
Jeans

Juice

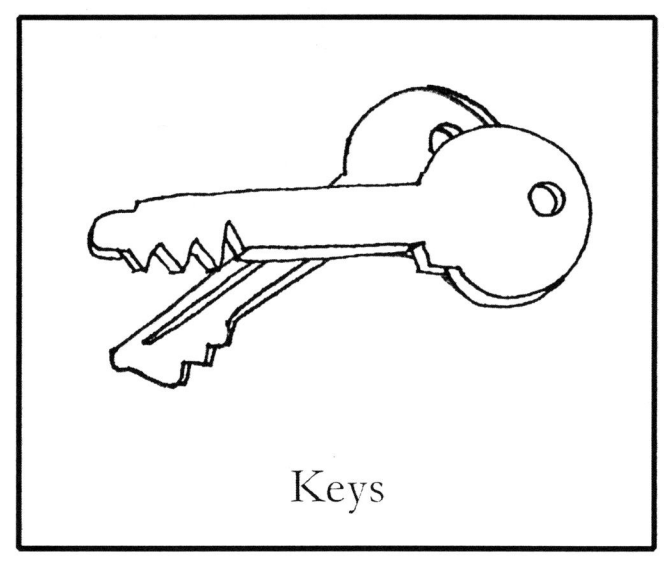
Keys

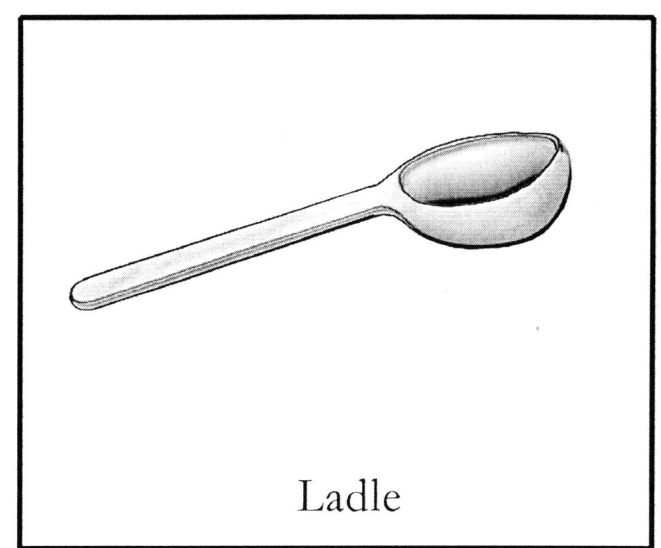
Ladle

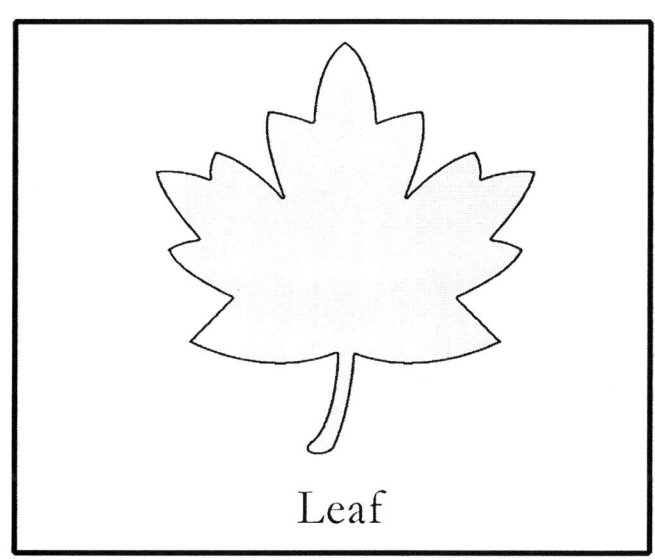
Leaf

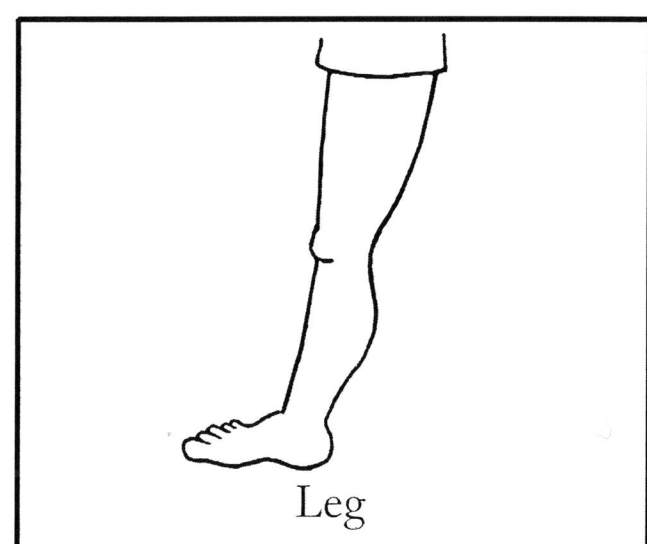
Leg

Nice

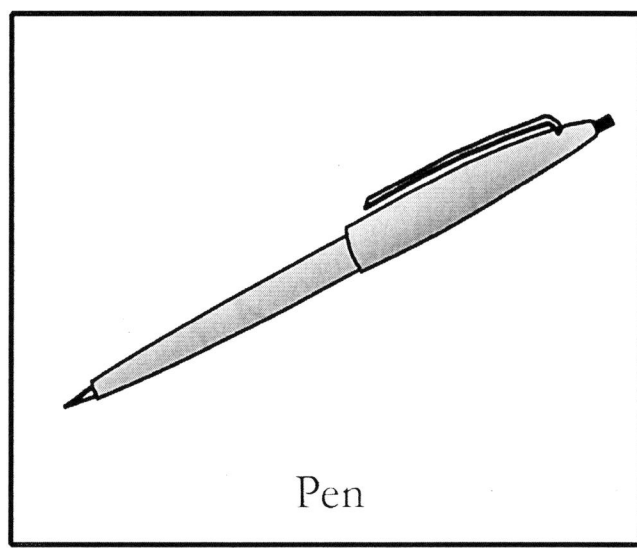
Pen

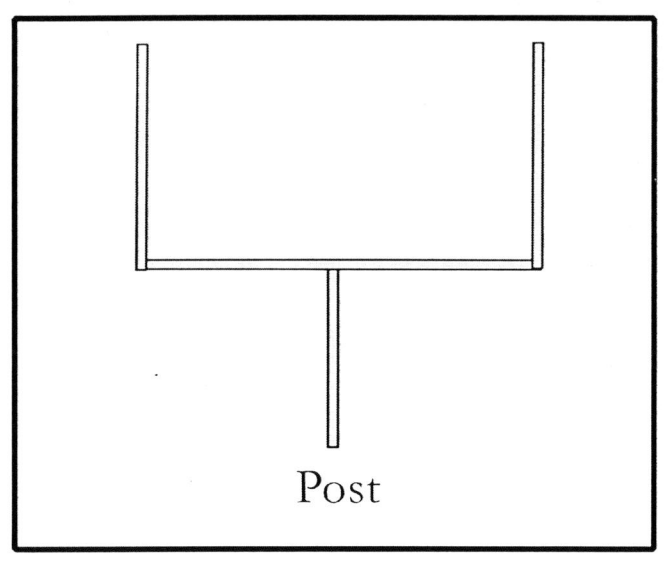

Post

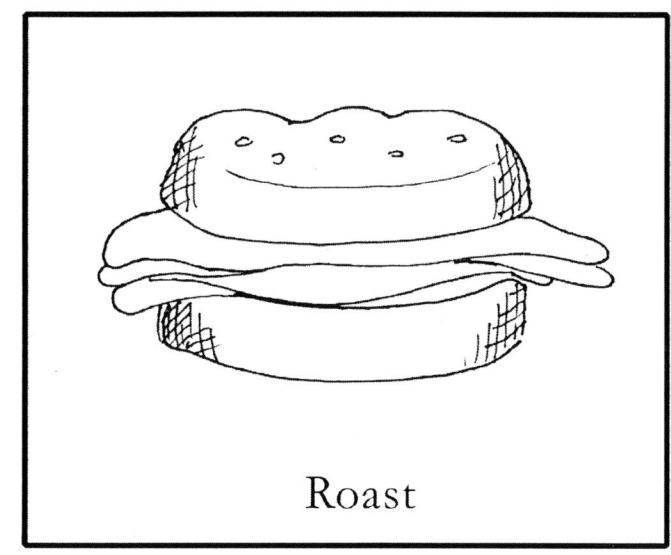

Roast

Rock

Rice

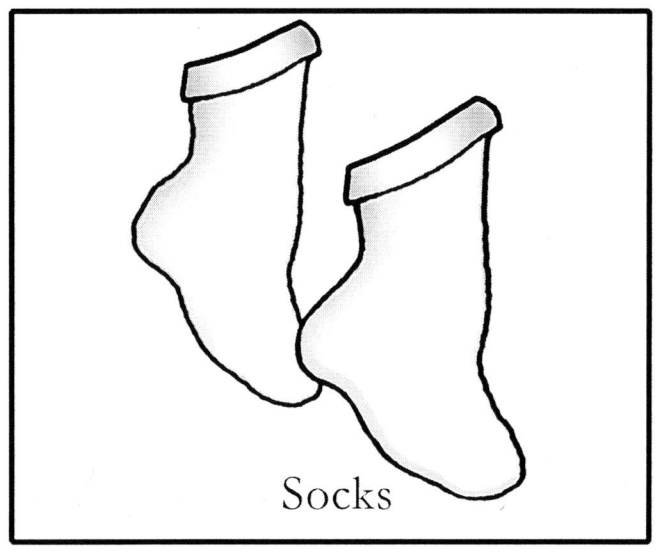

Socks

Sun

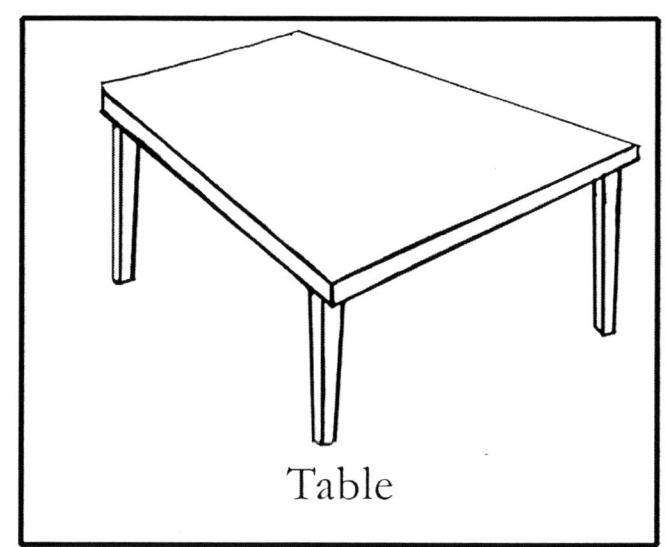
Table

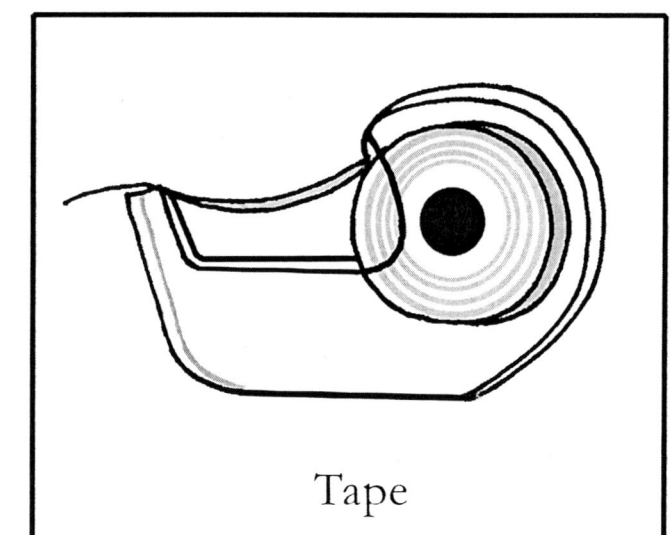
Tape

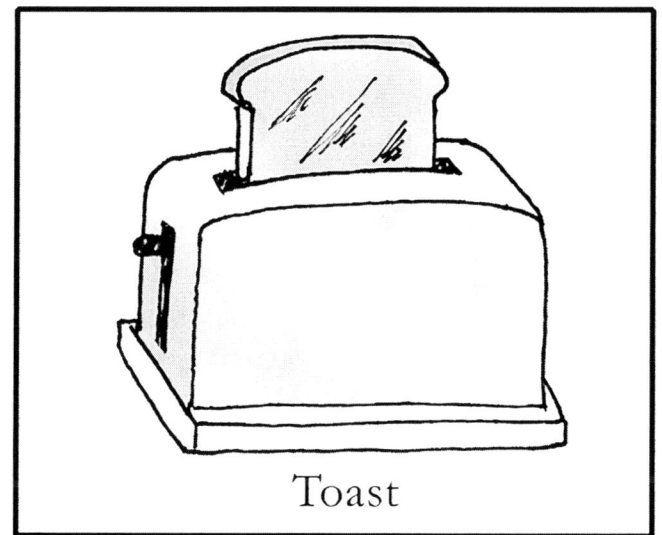
Toast

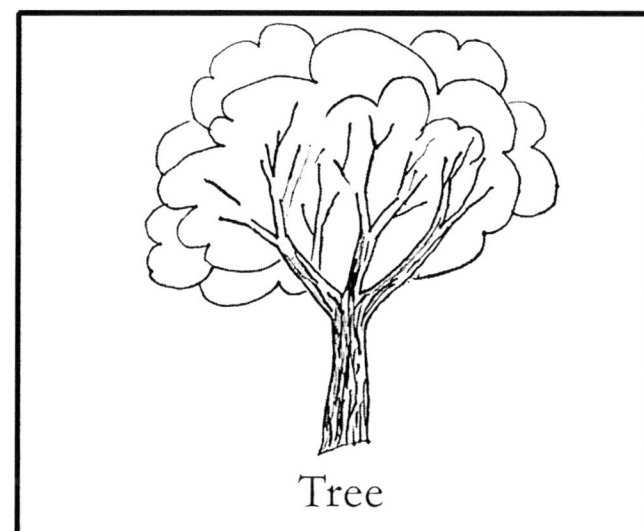
Tree

Red	Blue
Yellow	Green
Orange	Purple
White	Pink
Black	Brown
Gray	Gold

Big Cloud  Bigger Cloud  Biggest Cloud

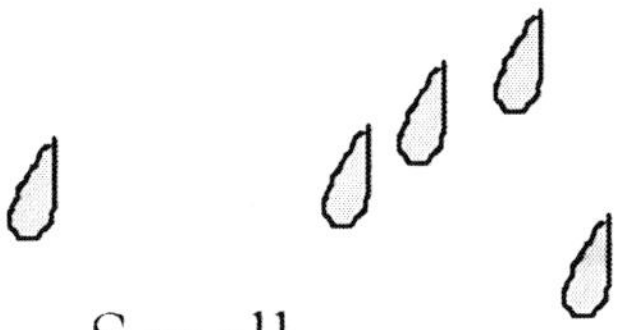

Small  Smaller  Smallest

Small Raincloud  Smaller Raincloud  Smallest Raincloud

Big Rainbow Bigger Rainbow  Biggest Rainbow

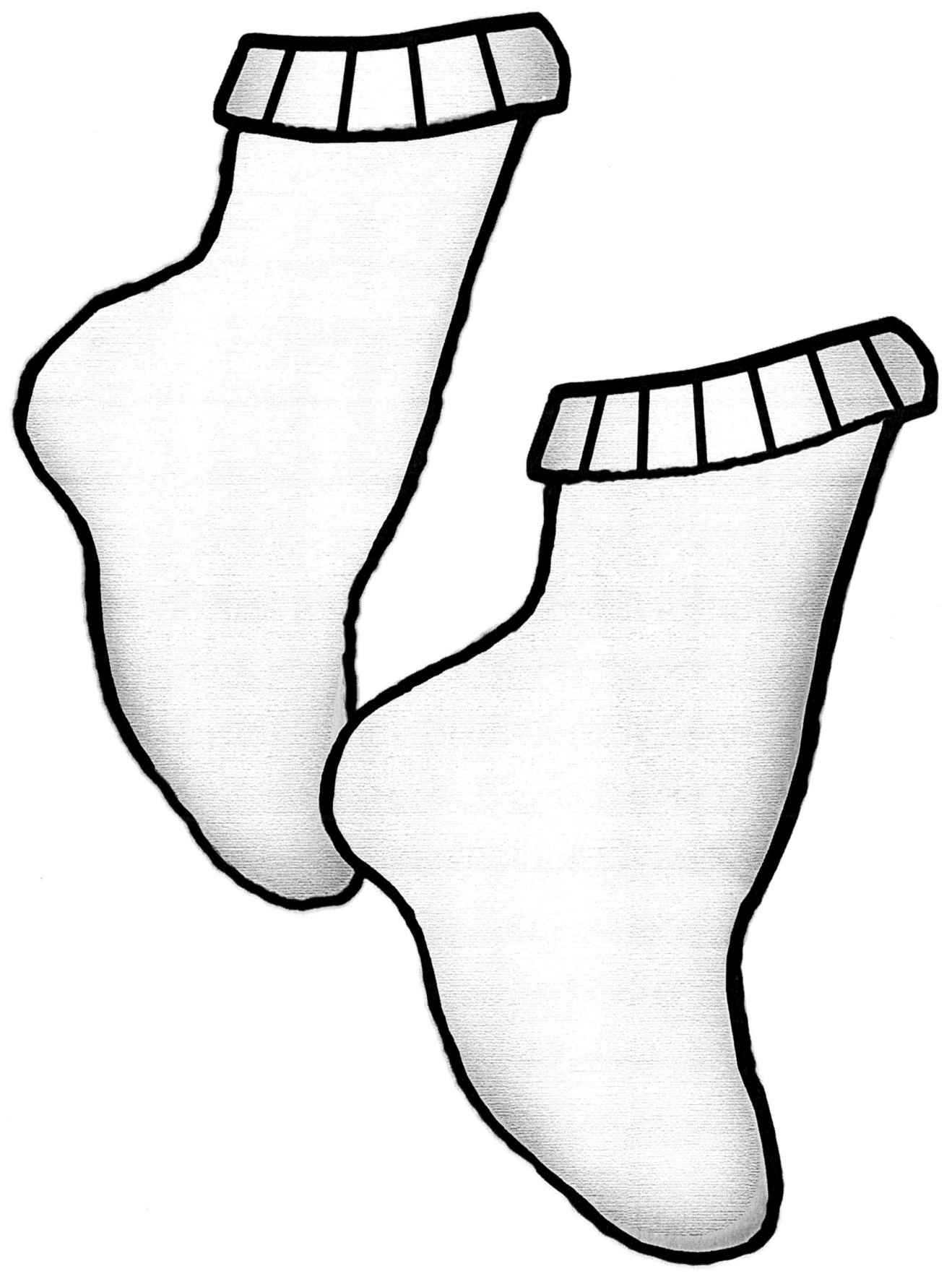

Pear

Bear

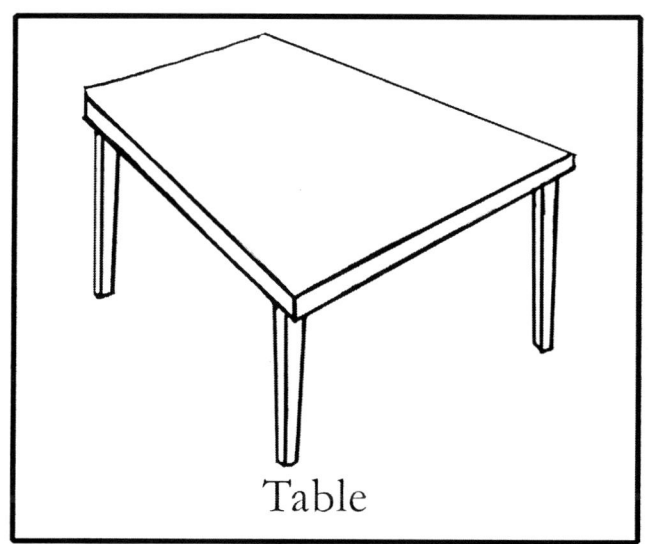
Table

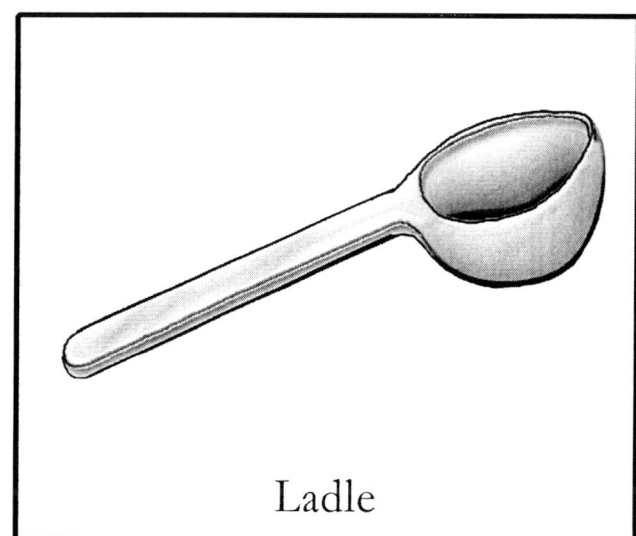
Ladle

Mable

Banana

Coconut

Snake

Cake

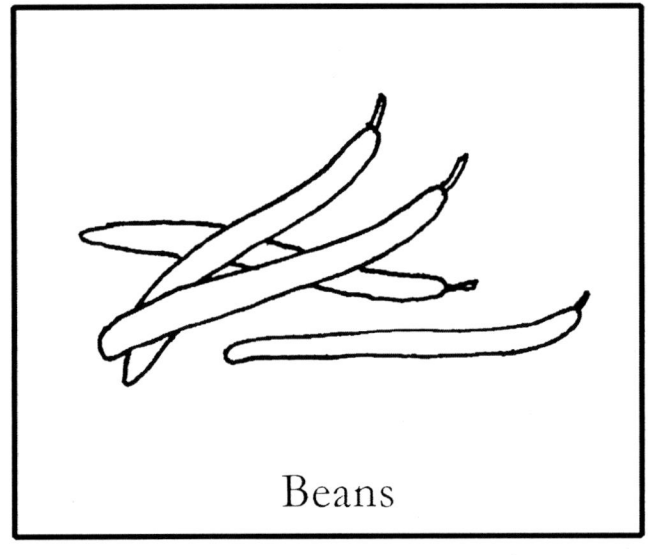
Beans

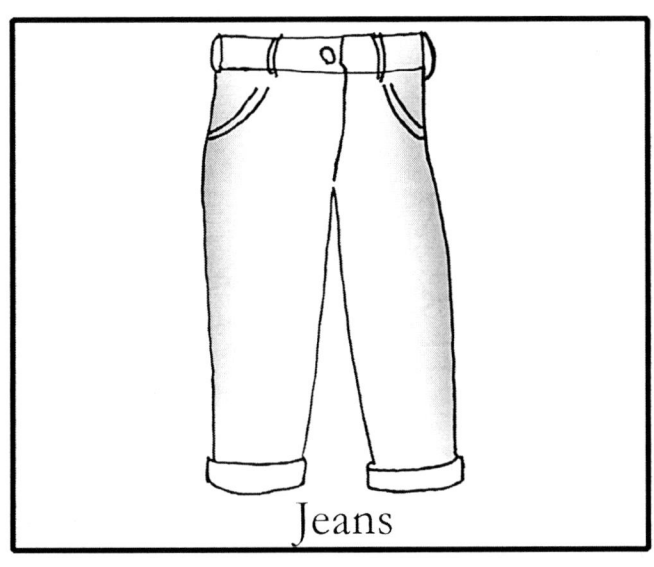
Jeans

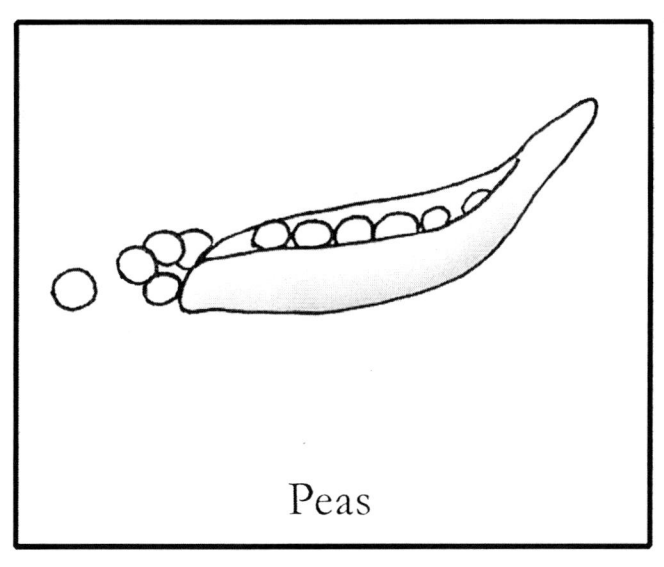

Peas

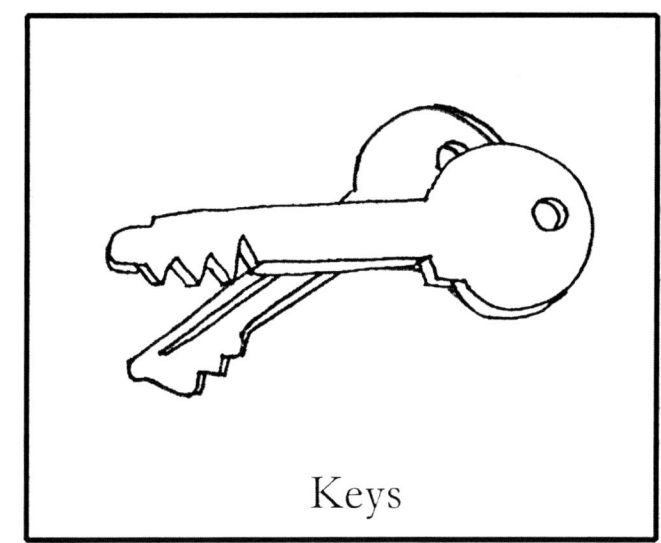

Keys

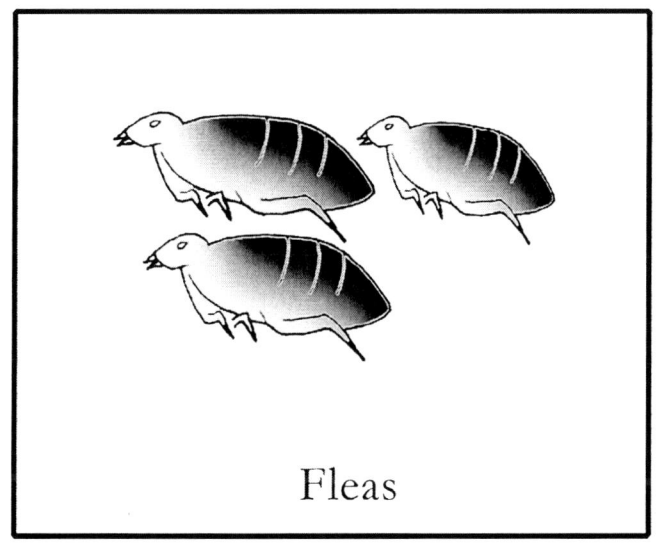

Fleas

Cheese

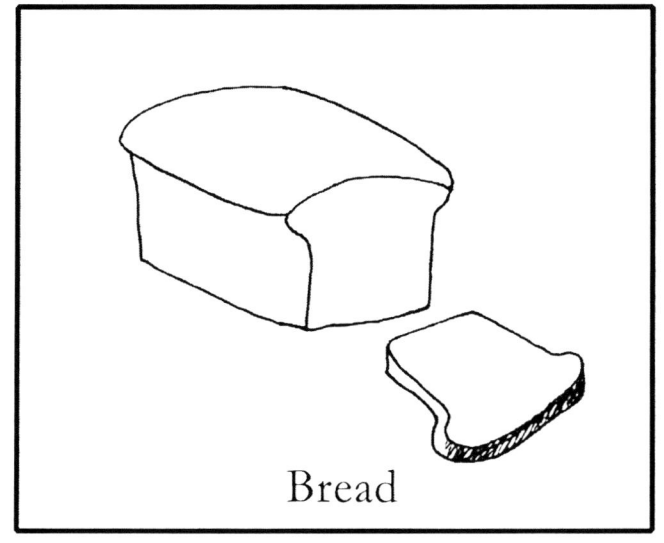

Bread

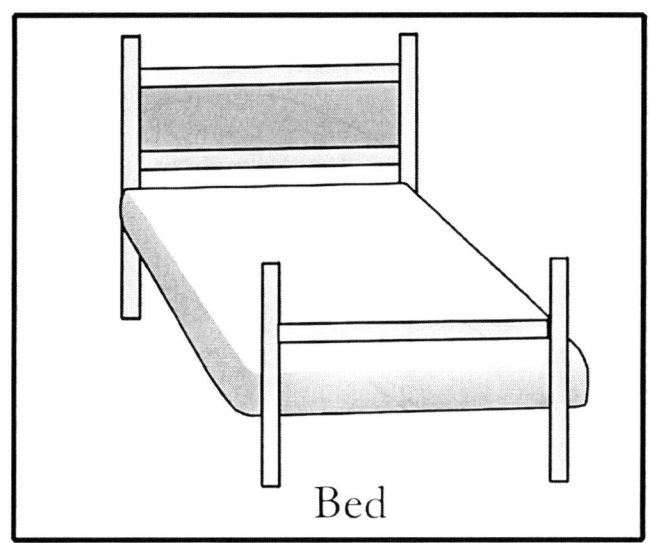

Bed

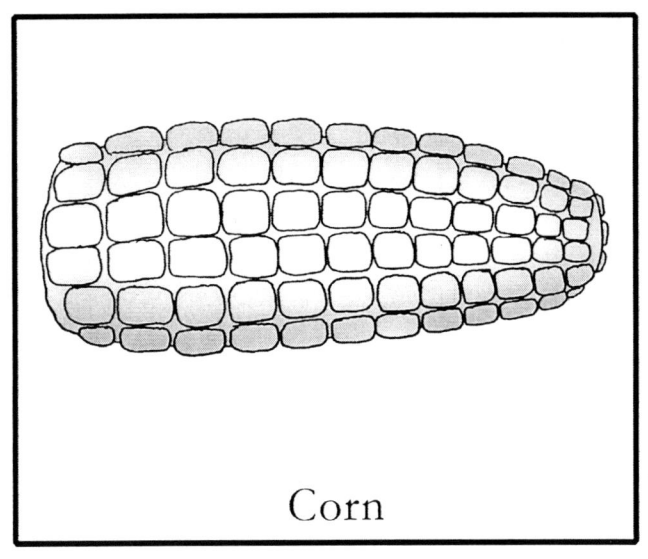
Corn

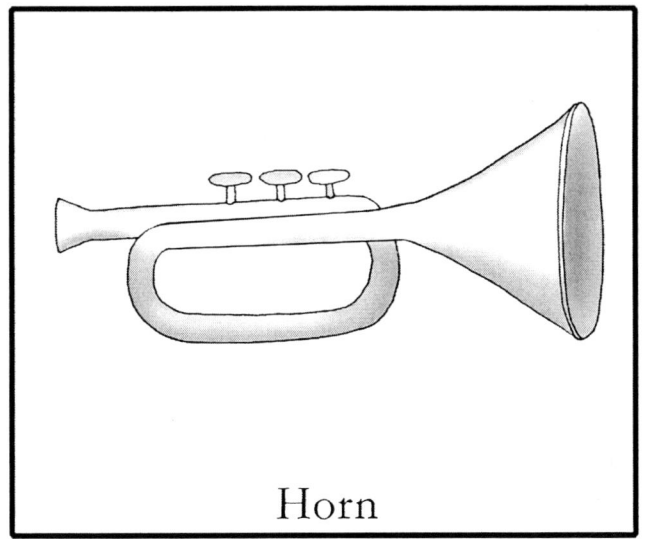
Horn

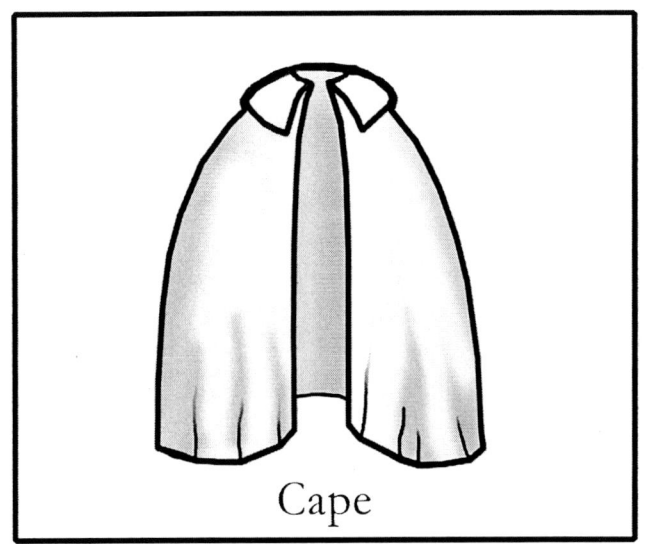
Cape

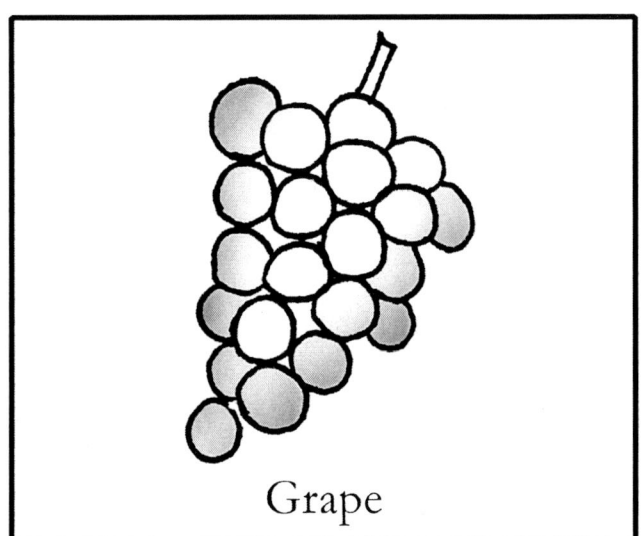
Grape

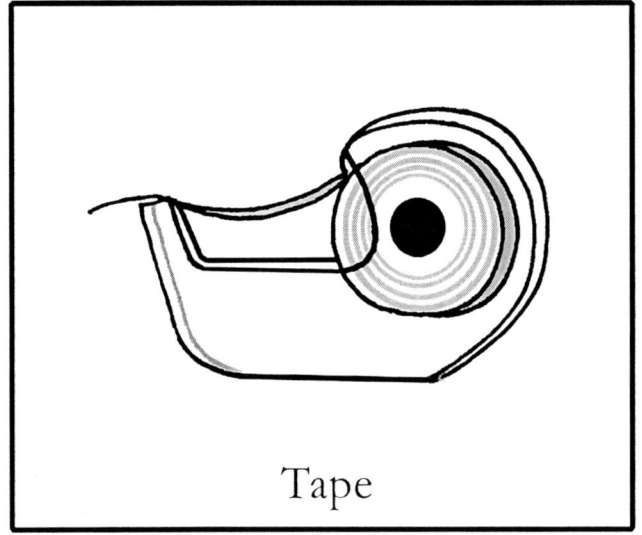
Tape

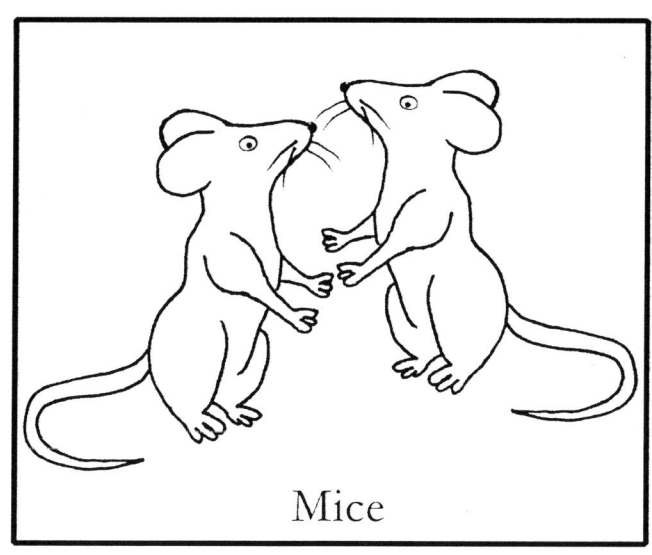
Mice

Rice

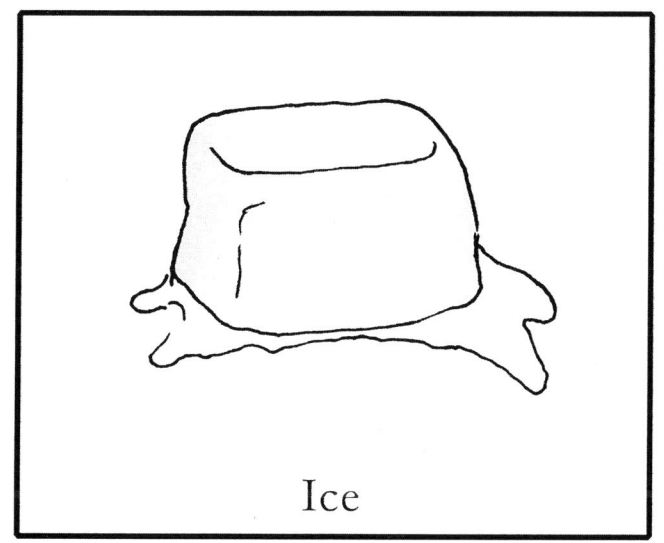
Ice

Nice

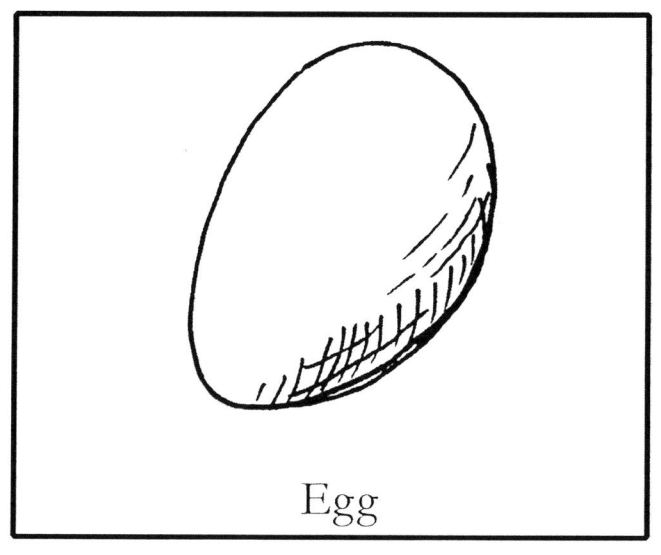
Egg

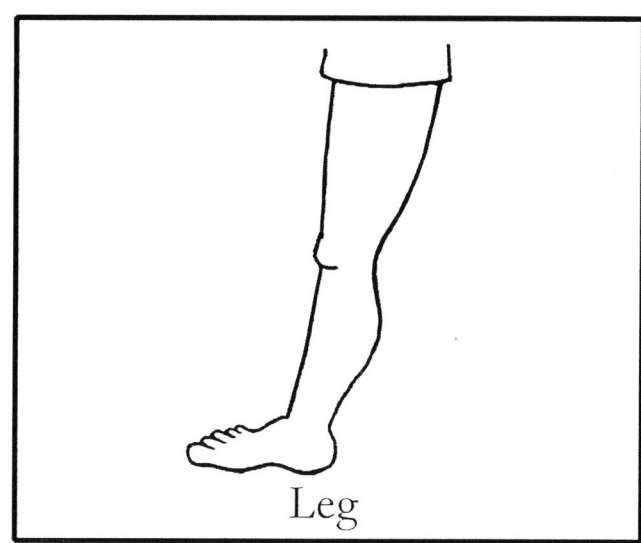
Leg

Clock

Blocks

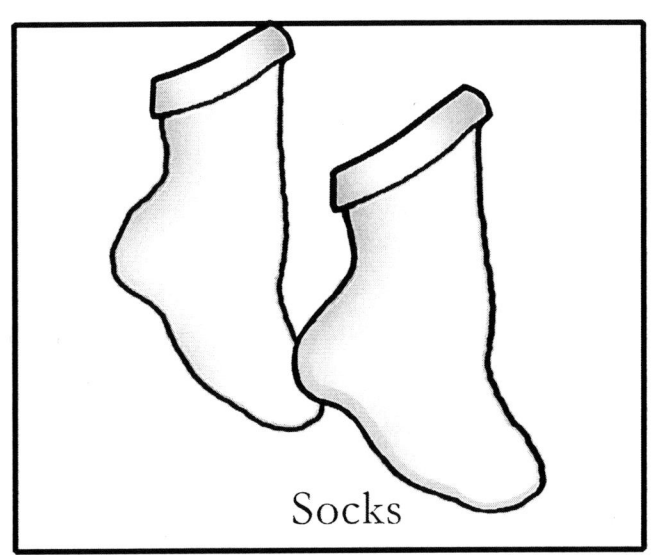
Socks

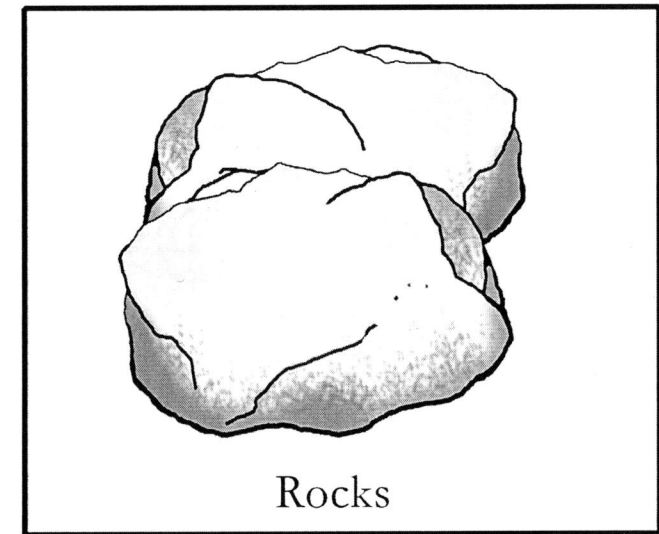
Rocks

Hen

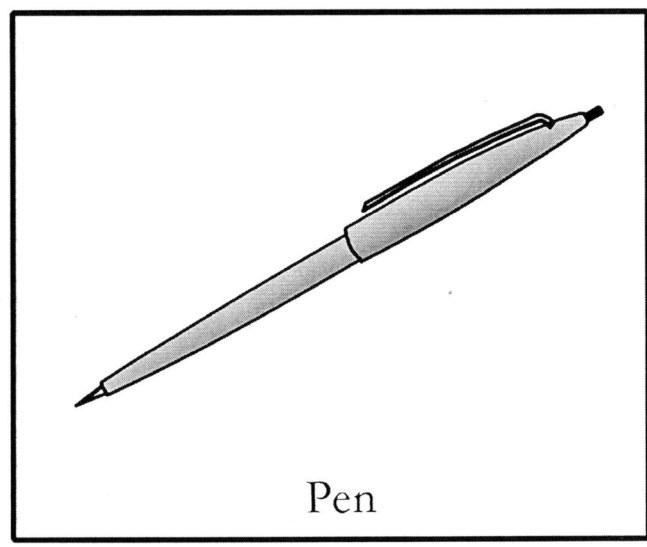
Pen

Ghost

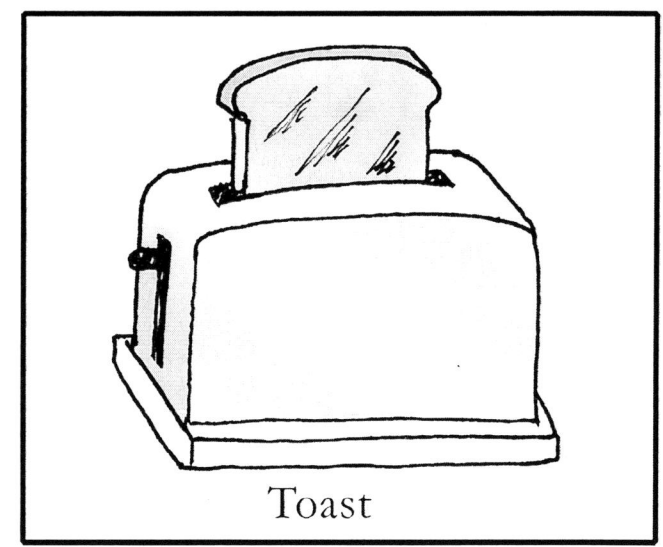
Toast

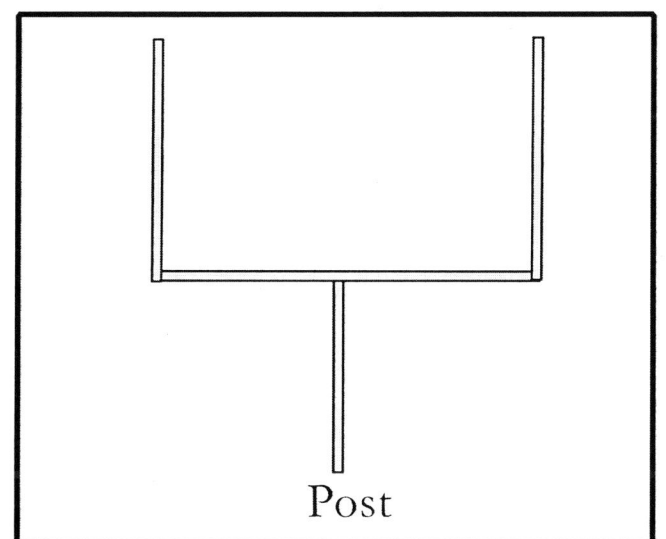
Post

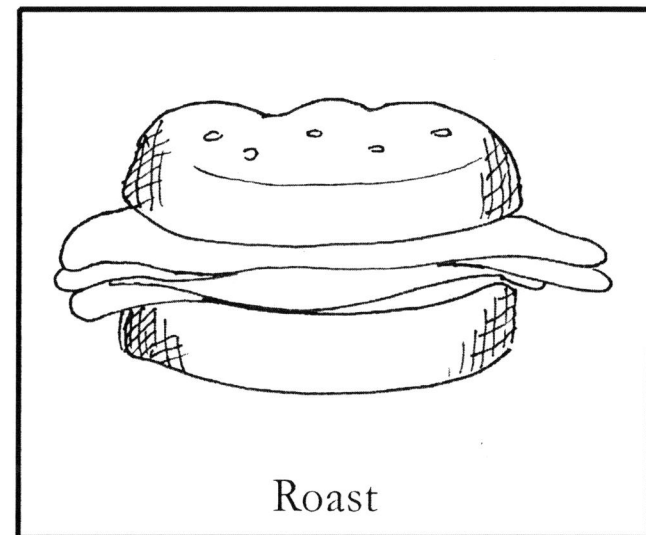
Roast

Frog

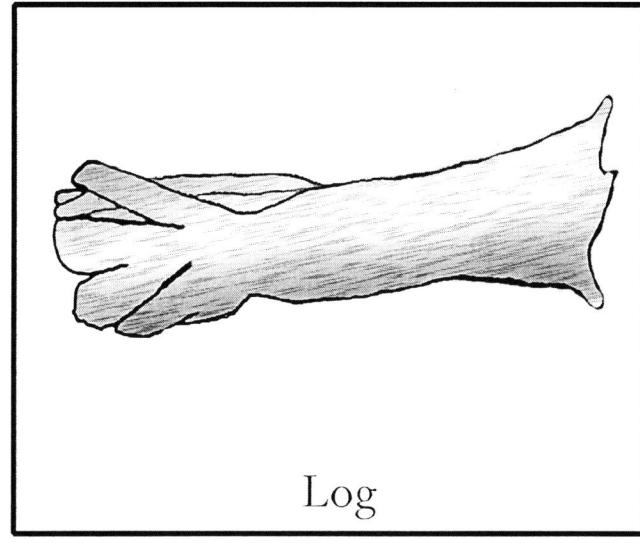
Log

Goat

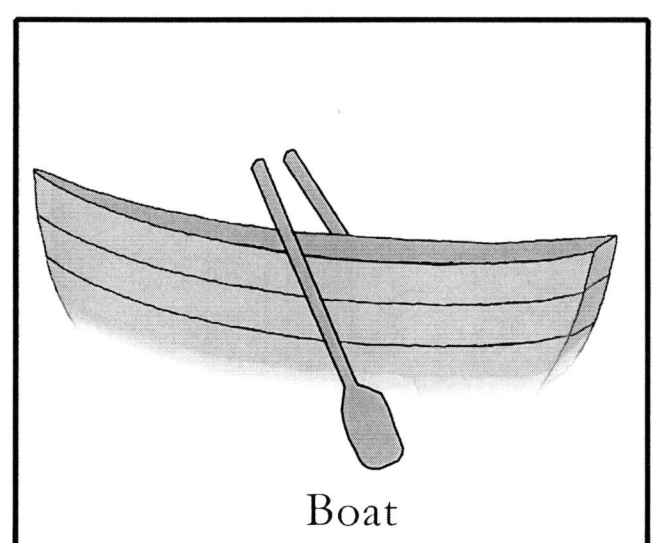
Boat

Goose

Moose

Juice

Monkey

Baboon

Cricket

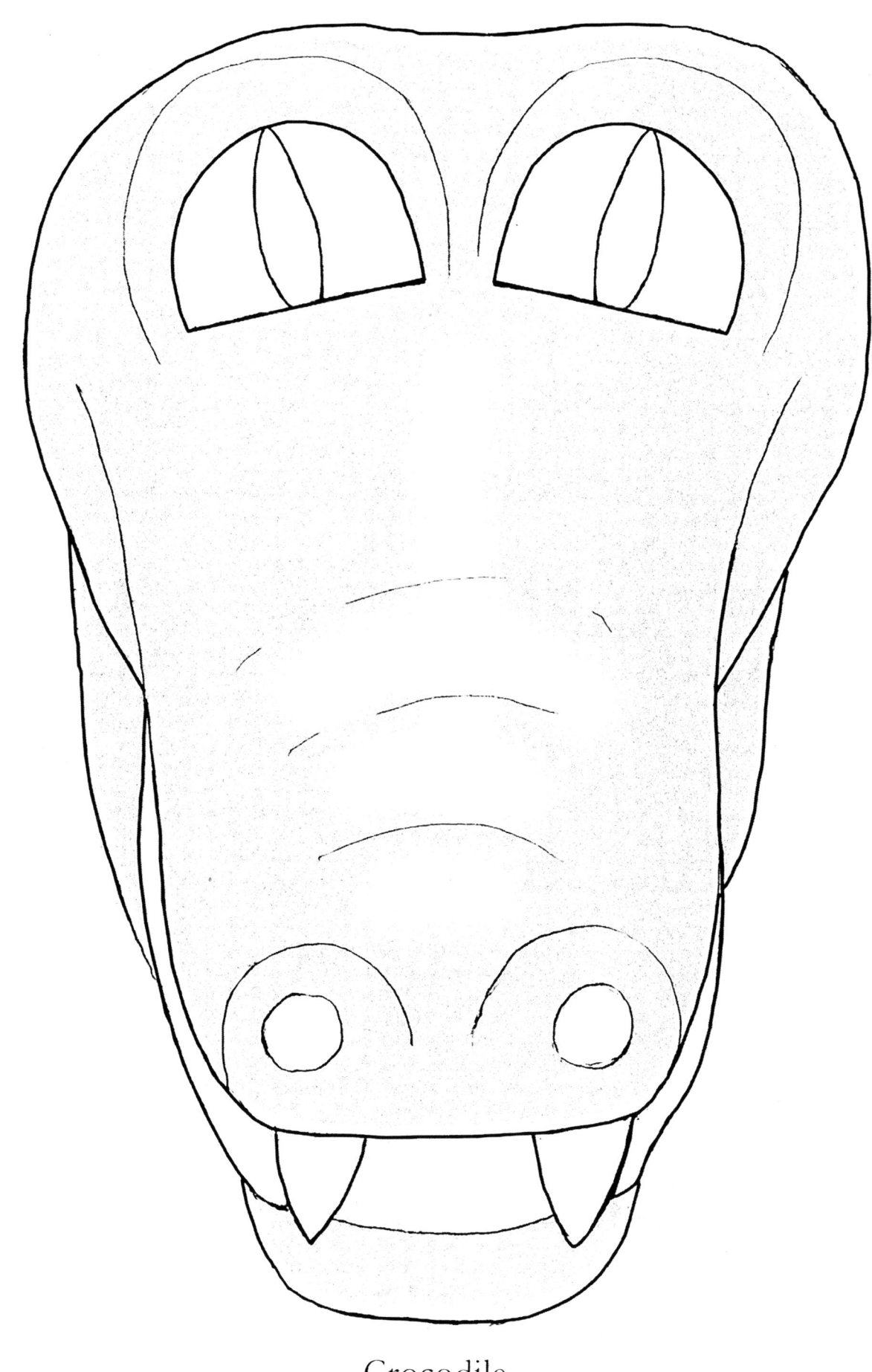

Crocodile

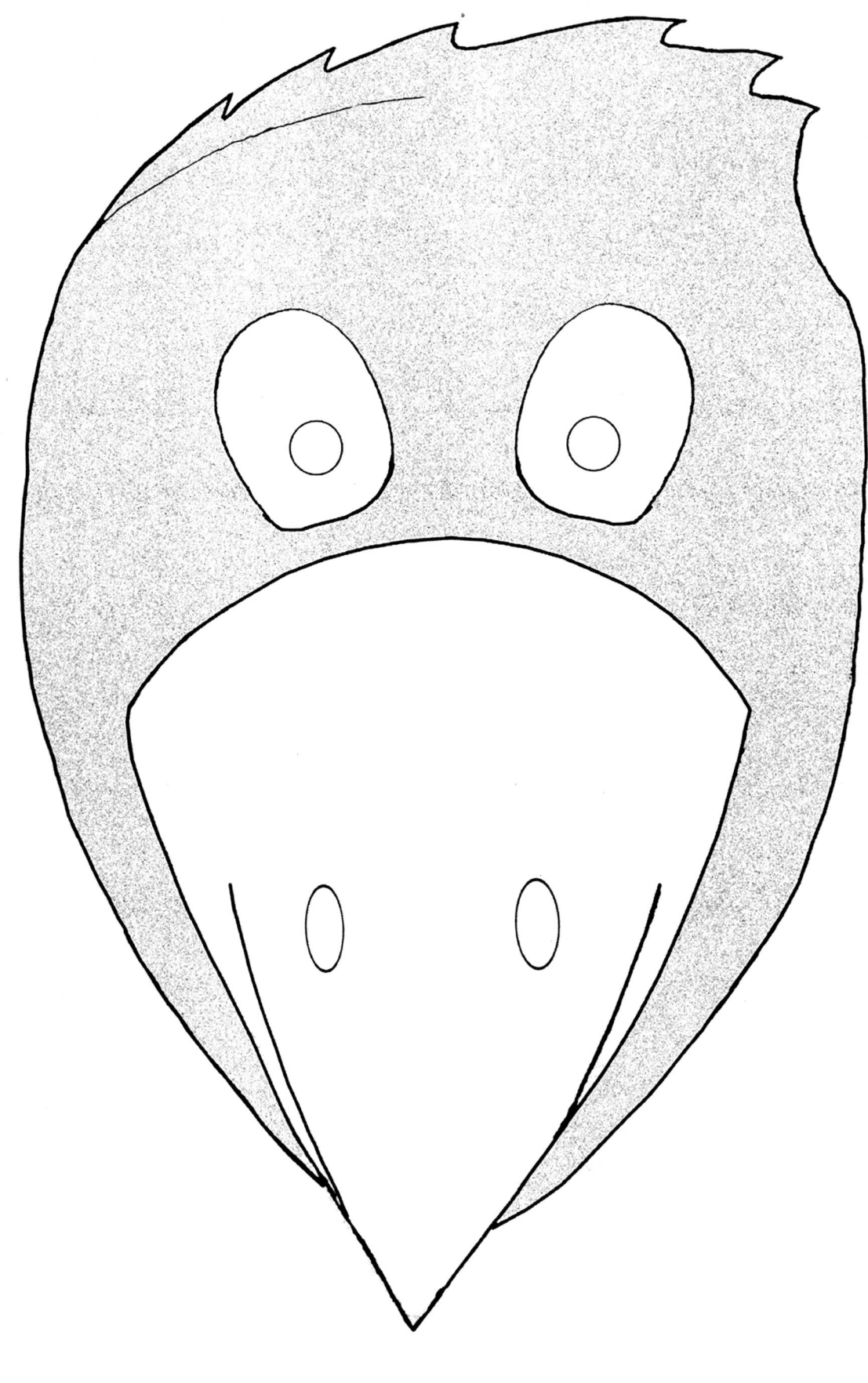
Crow

Dog

Fox

Frog

Goat

Hog

Mouse

Yak

Horse

Flutist

Baby

Cow

Dove

Ghost

Owl

Toucan